BLACK BEAR

The Spirit of the Wilderness

BLACK BEAR

The Spirit of the Wilderness

Barbara Ford

Illustrated with photographs

Houghton Mifflin Company   Boston   1981

Frontispiece:

A Vermont black bear. (Charles Willey, Vermont Fish and Game Department)

Library of Congress Cataloging in Publication Data
Ford, Barbara.
    Black bear, the spirit of the wilderness.
    SUMMARY: Discusses the black bear, North
America's smallest bear, the research being done
on it, and our responsibility for ensuring its
future.
        1. Black bear — Juvenile literature. [1. Black
bear. 2. Bears] I. Title.
QL737.C27F67   599.74'446   80-29227
ISBN 0-395-30444-X

Printed in the United States of America.
P 10 9 8 7 6 5 4 3 2 1

Contents

Acknowledgments

My special thanks to John O'Pezio of the New York State Department of Environmental Conservation and Michael R. Pelton of the University of Tennessee for helping me explore the subject of black bears. A number of other specialists also made vital contributions to my research. They are:

Gary L. Alt, Pennsylvania Game Commission
John J. Beecham, Idaho Department of Fish and Game
Gordon M. Burghardt, University of Tennessee
Thomas L. Burst, University of Tennessee
Tim Burton, California Department of Fish and Game
James E. Cardoza, Massachusetts Division of Fisheries and Wildlife
John M. Collins, North Carolina Wildlife Resources Commission
Bobby Conley, Arkansas Game and Fish Commission
Richard H. Conley, Tennessee Wildlife Resources Agency
Charles R. Dente, New York State Department of Environmental Protection
G. Edgar Folk, Jr., University of Iowa

Barrie K. Gilbert, Utah State University

Robert J. Hamilton, North Carolina Wildlife Resources Commission

Charles E. Hanson, The Museum of the Fur Trade

Stephen M. Herrero, University of Calgary

Roy Hugie, Maine Department of Inland Fisheries and Wildlife

Albert L. LeCount, Arizona Game and Fish Department

Frederick G. Lindzey, Utah State University

James S. Lindzey, Pennsylvania State University

Dennis Martin, Virginia Commission of Game and Inland Fisheries

Clifford J. Martinka, Glacier National Park

Ralph A. Nelson, University of Illinois–School of Clinical Medicine

Howard Quigley, University of Tennessee

Edward E. Reynolds, Modesto Junior College

Lynn L. Rogers, U.S. Forest Service

Jane Tate, University of Tennessee

David F. Taylor, Louisiana Department of Wildlife and Fisheries

Charles H. Willey, Vermont Fish and Game Department

The Morris County (N.J.) Free Library obtained a number of M.S. and Ph.D. theses for me via interlibrary loans. JoAnn Garrett of the Audubon Society of Missouri supplied a paper on the history of Missouri bears from the Society's back files.

BLACK BEAR

The Spirit of the Wilderness

CHAPTER I

The Black Bear Reveals Its Secrets

The female black bear raised her head to sniff the evening air. The delicious scent of decaying meat came to her sensitive nose. She got up from the leafy bed where she had spent the day resting with her two seven-month-old cubs and started off in the direction of the scent. The cubs padded after her. The bear family was in the Catskill Forest Preserve, a state-owned tract of 248,000 acres (99,200 hectares) in New York State's Catskill Mountains. The preserve is heavily wooded, with only a few roads and houses.

The bear's nose led her down a hill and into an area called Woodland Valley. Two nights before, one of the cubs, a 30-pound (13.5-kilograms) female, had had a strange experience in the valley. Her foot had been caught in a wire loop while she was hunting for food with her family. The snare held her captive overnight. The next morning, a man came up a hiking trail to the snare, weighed and measured the young bear, and then released her. She was frightened but unhurt. The mother bear had observed the incident but now she was leading her family back to Woodland Valley.

Before long, the mother had located the meat scent in a spot just off the hiking trail. It came from a large chunk of deer meat, which had been partially burned.

The meat lay on the ground at the small end of a V that had been formed out of logs; the same V-shaped arrangement of logs had existed at the site where the cub had been caught. The mother stepped up to the meat. Snap! A wire loop concealed beneath leaves tightened around the mother's ankle. She jerked her foot back but succeeded only in further tightening the wire, which was attached to a large tree.

When the mother bear found she could not get the wire off her ankle, she abandoned the snare and began chewing a nearby tree about five inches in diameter. Before the night was over, she had chewed it through with her strong teeth and the tree fell over. The cubs spent the night with their mother. A little after dawn, the same man who had released the young cub two nights before came up the hiking trail.

The female had been lying on her back, resting, when she smelled the human scent. She got up on all fours to face the man. The cubs ran off. The man approached the bear, then walked away. After visiting a number of empty snares similar to the one that had caught the female bear, he returned to a four-wheel-drive vehicle parked on an old logging road. He spoke into a citizens-band radio inside the vehicle.

"Tell John we've got an adult at the third set in the Valley," he said.

The black bear in the snare was about to become part of a research project that had been going on for nine years. In 1970, New York State's Big Game Unit, which is part of the Department of Environmental Conservation, began studying the black bear in the northern Catskill Mountains. Before 1970, the black-bear population in the area had been dropping; since

Tranquilized bear wearing a radio collar. (Lee Perry, Maine Fish and Game Department)

then, it has been fairly stable, at 250 to 300 bears. The Big Game Unit, which sets hunting regulations for bears and deer in New York, has changed the regulations several times in the Catskills in order to increase the bear population and then stabilize it at a higher level. In its research project, the Unit is trying to find out how many bears the northern Catskills can support.

The Big Game Unit's most important tool in studying bears is radio telemetry. Bears are captured with snares, a special collar is fitted on them, and then they are released. The collar has a transmitter that gives off a radio signal, which can be picked up with a special receiver and antennae. The bear can't hear the beeps.

The bears are usually tracked from a small airplane that carries antennae on its wings. More than 150 bears have been captured and about one-third of these have been fitted with radio collars and tracked. The other bears have been measured and marked with ear tags and tattoos.

By tracking bears, researchers in the Big Game Unit are learning, among other things, what kind of habitat, or living area, the black bear prefers in the Catskills. The results of the tracking program will be put together with the results of a land survey taken earlier to get this information; a computer will do much of the actual comparison work. Eventually, the Big Game Unit will identify additional areas that could support more black bears and then encourage the black-bear population to increase in those areas.

Habitat utilization is the most important aspect of the Catskill study, but the researchers are also obtaining other information about bears, such as their weights and ages.

The fall of 1979, when the female with the two cubs was captured, was probably the last year for capturing bears in the research project, although radio-collared bears will be tracked for several years more. Early one September morning in 1979, I drove to the northern Catskills to meet with John O'Pezio, the bear biologist for the Big Game Unit. O'Pezio had been trapping in the area for about a week, and expected to trap for two weeks more. A team of wildlife technicians and part-time assistants was working with him.

It was my first visit to the northern Catskills, although I had been to the southern Catskills when I lived in New York State. The southern Catskills have many hotels, campgrounds, restaurants, and cottages, so that I was struck by the wildness of the northern Catskills. For mile after mile, a winding road led through steep, heavily wooded hills with little sign of human habitation. Finally the road descended into a valley where a few rustic resorts were scattered. It was hard to believe the area was only a hundred miles from New York City. I parked at one of the resorts to wait for O'Pezio.

He arrived a short time later. "You picked a good week," he said. "We've captured a bear every day this week." He had already heard by CB radio from one of his assistants that there was an adult bear in one snare — the bear described at the opening of this chapter.

We got in O'Pezio's four-wheel-drive and drove to a nearby camp owned by Winnisook, Inc., a private club. The club allows the state bear researchers to use its facilities. There O'Pezio and John Palmateer, a wildlife technician, loaded equipment into the vehicle. Among the items they put in were radio collars, hypodermic needles, bottles of two different kinds of immobilizing drugs (drugs that work like an anesthetic), a tattooing kit, long poles, and a portable scale. The two men worked swiftly. "We don't like to leave bears in the snares any longer than we have to," said O'Pezio. "We check the snares first thing in the morning and get the bears early the same day."

Within a short time we were ready to go. I realized why we needed a four-wheel-drive when O'Pezio turned off the road onto a rutted logging track. The vehicle bounced and twisted as it made its way through the woods. The area we were driving through,

Researchers use a portable scale to weigh a bear. (University of Tennessee)

O'Pezio told me over the din, was part of the Catskill Forest Preserve. It occupies about forty per cent of the northern Catskills. The Preserve is heavily used by picnickers and hikers, but there are few encounters between people and bears.

"We took a survey a few years ago and sixty per cent of the people didn't even know there were bears here," said O'Pezio. "They thought we were trying to scare them."

Unlike some national parks, the Catskill Forest Preserve has never had a problem with bears that beg from people for food. O'Pezio thinks that bears in the Preserve do not make an association between human scent and food because there is little garbage or improperly stored food. Also, the number of bears is kept in balance with the amount of natural food by bear hunting. The bears have plenty to eat without looking for artificial food. Occasionally, a bear will raid garbage cans or a campground, but people in the area do not get too excited about it. "People here tolerate bears," commented O'Pezio.

O'Pezio stopped the vehicle and he and Palmateer each grabbed some of the equipment and started off at a quick pace up a sloping trail. I hurried after them. When we got near the area where the snared bear was located, the two men went ahead to check out the situation. They came back in a few minutes.

"She's there," said O'Pezio. "I think we heard a cub running away, too." He turned to Palmateer. "One hundred thirty."

"One hundred fifty," said Palmateer.

O'Pezio wrote the estimated weights in a notebook. Then he took one of the poles, fitted a hypodermic needle into the top, and loaded the needle with fluid from one of the bottles of drugs.

"What we do," he explained as he worked, "is have each of the crew estimate the bear's weight by looking at it, then we average the estimates. We use an amount of immobilizing drug based on the average estimate." The drug he was using that day is called M99, or Etorphine. The advantages of M99 are that it is very safe to use and it has an effective antidote, which can get the tranquilized bear back on its feet within a few minutes after the drug has been given.

O'Pezio put a stethoscope around his neck. He took one pole and Palmateer took the other. I followed them for a few hundred feet. Suddenly I spotted the bear through the trees. She gave a jump or two when she saw us, but seemed quite calm for the situation she was in. She made no noise at all. O'Pezio moved to the rear of the bear. Palmateer approached her head. He teased the bear with his pole, distracting her, while O'Pezio used his syringe to push the needle into her rump. It was all over in less than a minute. Within another minute, the bear lay down. She got up, then lay down again.

When I stood next to the unconscious animal, I could see that her front leg was inside a loop of cable wire attached to a tree. The device is called the Aldrich foot snare, after the professional bear hunter from Washington State who invented it. When a bear steps on a trigger in the snare, the loop of wire is thrown over its leg and pulled tight. Most bear researchers now use the Aldrich snare because it is lightweight, doesn't harm bears, and is safe to use around other wildlife and people.

O'Pezio picked up the bear's foot to show me that

Howard Quigley of the University of Tennessee shows the two kinds of capture devices used in bear research. *Left:* Aldrich foot snare. *Right:* culvert or barrel trap, with door that falls when animal steps inside.

John O'Pezio checks heartbeat of Number 146.

there was no injury to it. "We've never had a bear seriously hurt with this snare," he said.

He lifted the unconscious bear up in his arms and lowered her onto a plastic sheet he had put on the forest floor. Then he crouched beside her and listened to her heartbeat with the stethoscope, to see how the drug was affecting her. M99 slows breathing and increases heart rate; if either process becomes too abnormal, the antidote is administered immediately. In this case, everything was satisfactory. O'Pezio checked the heartbeat and breathing several more times while the men were working on the animal. "A lactating female," said Palmateer, squeezing a drop of milk out of one of the bear's nipples. "She's got cubs around somewhere."

The first thing the men did with the bear was take six measurements, beginning with head length and ending with body weight. To weigh her, they lifted the animal in a rope bag attached to a portable scale.

"One hundred twenty-six and seven-tenths," said Palmateer.

After the measurements, O'Pezio propped the bear's mouth open and pulled out two small premolar teeth. They came out easily. Their loss, O'Pezio pointed out to me, does not bother the bear. Next he tattooed a number inside the bear's lip with a needle from the tattooing kit. The tattoo included the figure *146*, for the 146th bear the New York State team has marked in the Catskill area. If the bear is recaptured or killed, she can be identified by means of the tattoo. Earlier, they had put a stainless-steel tag in the animal's ear, also for identification.

The last step was the radio collar. "Twenty inches," said O'Pezio after measuring the bear's neck. "We'll give her two inches for growth. Her teeth are worn and it's my guess that she's old enough so she won't grow much larger." He took out the radio collar, a sturdy nylon band weighing about two pounds, including the radio transmitter. Before he put it on, he affixed a small metal plate to it. On the plate is a message offering a twenty-five-dollar reward to anyone who returns the collar if it drops off or the bear is killed. He closed the collar by bolting it with a huge pair of pliers and cut off the excess piece.

Finally, O'Pezio administered the antidote with a needle. After a minute or two, the bear breathed more deeply. Five minutes later, her ears twitched. Seconds after that, she was up and running away without a backward glance.

The whole procedure had taken about forty minutes, a little longer than usual. When he works with two assistants, O'Pezio explained, it takes less time.

On our way out of the woods, we passed another trap on the same line, this one undisturbed. A smelly chunk of deer meat was still sitting on the ground above the snare. The meat is burned with a torch, O'Pezio remarked, to make its odor even stronger. The snare was enclosed by two low walls made out of branches and brush that came to a V behind the snare. The bear walks into the wide part of the V and is led up to the brush-covered snare.

To me, the snare setup looked obvious, but not to bears, apparently. On this particular trap line, bears had been caught frequently.

The next day, in a heavy rainstorm, I watched O'Pezio and other members of the New York State team drug two more snared bears, both less than two years old. Black bears usually do not mature until they are three to four years old, so these bears were sub-adults, or "yearlings." Each weighed less than 100 pounds. Unlike the adult female I had seen the day before, these bears were nervous about the situation in which they found themselves. When they spotted us, they leaped around in an agitated way until the drug took effect.

The second yearling, a female that later turned out to weigh just 66 pounds (29.9 kilograms) took a long time to become unconscious. At one point, she began tossing branches our way. Finally, however, she put her head down on a log and went to sleep.

"Smaller bears tend to be more active in the snares," O'Pezio remarked as we watched the young female bounding around attached to her snare.

During this capture we were accompanied by a resident of the area, who lived in a house at the bottom of the hill. Although the bear was snared less than a mile from his house, he said he had never seen a bear in the Catskills before. That afternoon, after I left, O'Pezio and his team captured and drugged still another year-ling on the same trap line where the adult had been taken the day before. The total of three bears captured in a single day ties the record for the Catskill team.

Bears, as one of the Catskills researchers told me, seem to move around more when it rains, making it more likely that they will step into one of the snares.

When O'Pezio got back from the Catskills to the Big Game Unit's Delmar office (near Albany), he gave the bear teeth he had collected to Bruce Weber, a wildlife technician. After soaking them in acid to remove the calcium, Weber froze the softened teeth and cut very thin slices from them with a microtome (the micro-tome is an instrument that functions like a slicing ma-chine). The slices were stained with a dye to make them easier to "read," and put on slides. Under a mi-croscope, rings on the cementum, the material that holds the tooth root to the gum, could be seen. Each ring stands for a year in the life of a bear.

The procedure is known as the "cementum annuli" technique, *annuli* being the Latin word for rings. For most large wild animals, it is the most accurate way of telling age. The adult female I had seen turned out to be twelve and three-quarters, an old age for a wild black bear.

The age of a wild animal is important to biologists such as John O'Pezio, because it indicates how the pop-ulation of the species is faring. If most of the black bears in an area are below the age of maturity, with very few older animals, the population is probably de-clining. This is happening in a few sections of the East. If, on the other hand, there are many young animals but also older ones spread through all age groups, the population may well be increasing. In the northern Catskills, bears come from all age groups, a good indication that the population is stable. In 1979, for instance, two very old bears, one eighteen, the other nineteen, were killed by cars in the northern Catskills. The average age of the bears in that area is three and a half to four years.

Charles R. Dente, one of the wildlife technicians who works with John O'Pezio, kept me informed as to what happened to Number 146 after she was radio-collared. In late October, six weeks after she had been captured, an airplane piloted by another wildlife technician, Chuck Hackford, picked up the bear's radio signals at Traver Hollow, three miles west of where she was captured. A week later, she had journeyed a half mile northwest to Cross Mountain. The next time she was located, in early December, she was a mile and a half north, at South Mount Pleasant. By mid-December, she was three-quarters of a mile north, in North Mount Pleasant, near the town of Mount Tremper.

The Big Game Unit team thought Number 146 was likely to make her den at this last spot. O'Pezio and the technicians planned to visit the den and radio-collar her yearlings, who would also be in the den. One of the yearlings was believed to be the cub caught two days before Number 146.

Number 146's cubs would be yearlings when they left the den in the spring of 1980. In late spring or early summer, the family would split up and the young bears would strike out on their own. The period after the family breakup is the most crucial period in the life of a young black bear. By radio-collaring Number 146's cubs, the Big Game Unit hoped to find out more about how young bears behave at this time, and how they go about establishing themselves in a new area.

The Catskill project I watched in operation for a brief period is just one of a number of black-bear studies being carried out in the United States today. Like O'Pezio and his team, biologists and technicians in other parts of the country are capturing black bears, drugging them, and fitting them out with radio collars. They, too, take measurements and blood samples. Later, the radio-collared bears are tracked from the ground or from the air. In the winter, researchers enter bear dens to take more measurements and radio-collar yearling cubs. Additional research is aimed at obtaining information on such subjects as why bears mark trees and how they see objects. There is an explosion of black-bear research.

Why this sudden interest in an animal that has occupied the North American continent since long before humans arrived?

In the 1960s, scientists interested in American wildlife began to realize that the black bear, the most numerous and widespread bear in North America, was in a decline in many areas. Since the mid-nineteenth century, bears have vanished altogether in some Eastern and Midwestern states. In the twentieth century, their numbers have dropped even in Eastern states where they had been fairly numerous. After 1950 in a few areas, the decline accelerated, even though bears were being given more protection.

To save the black bear in areas where the species is declining and to keep its numbers stable in other areas, scientists needed information about the animal and its habits. Before the 1960s, however, few people had studied the black bear, and very little was known about it. Because the black bear lives alone in heavy woods or swamps, avoiding people if at all possible, it is difficult to observe the animal with conventional methods. But by the 1960s, a number of new research tools had become available to prospective bear researchers. These tools make it possible to obtain information from free-ranging black bears without actually watching them.

The most important new tool is radio telemetry. It was first employed for free-roaming hoofed animals, but its usefulness for black bears, too, soon became apparent. Dr. Lynn L. Rogers, of the U.S. Forest Service — who wrote his doctoral thesis at the University of Minnesota on black bears — points out that this bear is big enough to carry a sizable transmitter, which can give signals for at least a year. After the bear enters its den and goes into hibernation, the collar can be changed to allow room for growth, and any yearling cubs can be collared, too. This means bears can be tracked for virtually their entire life, a procedure Rogers carried out with several animals over a nine-year period. Researchers such as Rogers have been able to obtain information from radio-collared bears on habitat, home ranges, activity patterns, denning areas, social behavior, and food preferences, among other subjects.

Telemetry is an invaluable aid to black-bear researchers, but some other new techniques are important, too. One is the cementum-annuli procedure, which, like telemetry, was first worked out with wild animals other than the bear; before its development, estimating the age of many animals was largely a mat-

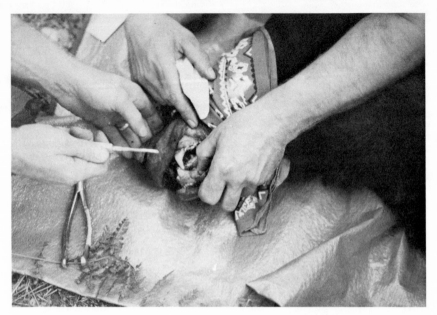

O'Pezio and Palmateer pull a premolar tooth from Number 146.
Below: cross section of a tooth from a New York State bear reveals
that it was almost twelve years old. Each layer indicates one year.
(John O'Pezio)

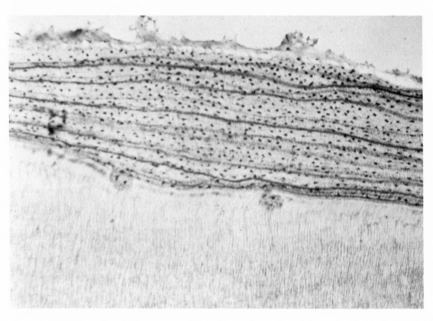

ter of guesswork. At first, bear researchers used the canine teeth in the cementum-annuli process. These are the sharp, pointed teeth at the corners of the jaw. But canine removal created problems. Not only are the teeth hard to remove, but bear hunters — who supply some of the teeth researchers use — prefer mounted trophies with the mouth open in a fierce snarl; with a canine removed, the snarl is not nearly so menacing. In addition, canines cannot be removed from live bears, because these teeth are necessary for eating.

In the late 1960s, New York State researchers and others developed a method for using premolars for the aging of bears. These are the small, easy-to-extract teeth at the side of the bear's jaw. The premolar can be removed from a live animal without affecting the animal's ability to eat food, and the tooth's loss is unnoticeable in mounted trophies. Charles Willey, a Vermont state biologist, described this method in a scientific journal in 1974. The Willey technique works well unless the bear is very old, which makes the annual rings hard to read. In aging dead bears that are believed to be very old, a canine tooth is usually pulled along with the premolar, and a false canine is substituted if the bear is wanted as a trophy.

The use of tools such as these has been made possible by another development: safe, effective immobilizing drugs. (These drugs are sometimes called tranquilizing drugs, although their real function is to put the bear to sleep.) There are obvious problems with handling a big, strong animal such as the black bear, but today's drugs make the job fairly routine. No researcher has been seriously injured in carrying out research on a tranquilized bear. Only a few bears have died accidentally from drugs, and the vast majority seem to suffer no ill effects. Some individual bears have been drugged more than once in a single year without problems. The existence of antidotes for drugs such as M99 makes the drugging procedure even safer.

Black-bear research projects employing radio collars and other new tools are under way today in at least a dozen states, including Arizona, California, Florida, Idaho, Maine, Minnesota, Pennsylvania, and Washington. Georgia, North Carolina, and Tennessee are cooperating in an effort funded by the federal government; the borders of these Southern states touch, so that the same population of bears roams the Appalachian Mountain region in all three states. Most of the workers involved in black-bear research are employed by state governments, but some are on the faculties of colleges and universities.

A black bear is big enough to carry a transmitter that can give signals for at least a year. Portable receiver on right.

The most comprehensive black-bear research program in the country is being conducted at the University of Tennessee in Knoxville, under the direction of Dr. Michael R. Pelton, of the department of forestry. At any one time, half a dozen of Pelton's graduate students are investigating black bears in Great Smoky Mountains National Park, which lies about twenty miles from the campus. The park is believed to have between 450 and 600 bears. When I visited the university in the summer of 1979, Pelton's students were studying bear habitat, tree marking, and reproduction, among other topics. Jane Tate, a Ph.D. candidate, had just finished her research on the Smokies' famous "panhandler" bears, which beg food from tourists. The University of Tennessee participates in the three-state program mentioned above.

The black bear still hasn't yielded all its secrets, but thanks to the efforts of modern researchers, we now know far more about it than we did ten years ago. The new knowledge may help save the animal for future generations of Americans.

CHAPTER II

The Black Bear's Vital Statistics

Probably the first thing most people notice about any bear is its size. Black bears are the smallest bears in North America but they are sizable creatures, particularly compared with most wild animals in the United States. Full-grown males average 250 to 350 pounds (113 to 158 kilograms), females 120 to 180 pounds (54 to 82 kilograms). Sub-adult males aged a year to a year and one-half weigh about the same as the smaller adult females, 100 to 150 pounds (45 to 68 kilograms). A male usually reaches its maximum weight at age five or six, a female at age four or five.

The largest known black bear in this country was a male shot by a hunter in New York State in 1975. It weighed 750 pounds (340 kilograms), as much as the average male grizzly bear. Other record-setting black-bear males in the United States have weighed, respectively, 725 pounds, 720 pounds, 690 pounds, 671 pounds, and 660 pounds (or 329, 327, 313, 304, and 299 kilograms). Females never even approach these weights, although some unusual individuals have scaled over 300 pounds (136 kilograms).

In some areas of the United States, black bears grow unusually large. New York's Adirondack Mountains are noted for big bears. Besides the 750-pound record set-ter just mentioned, New York had a 660-pound (299-kilogram) bear taken by a hunter in the Adirondacks in 1974. A bear weighing more than 700 pounds was killed in Wisconsin in 1963 and another Wisconsin bear killed the same year was only a little smaller. Virginia and Pennsylvania both have two bears weighing over 600 pounds on their record books. Most record-setting bears have come from Eastern states and there is other evidence that Eastern black bears tend to be larger than Western ones. In Great Smoky Mountains National Park, the biggest bear captured by Michael Pelton and his students weighed 510 pounds (230 kilograms). A Minnesota bear captured by Lynn Rogers weighed 539 pounds (244 kilograms). By contrast, the largest bear in a recent California study weighed just 324 pounds (147 kilograms).

Bears that live in parks are heavier than bears outside parks. Biologist David Graber, of the University of California, who studied black bears in California's Yosemite Park, found a number of males weighing well over 400 pounds and many females close to 300 pounds. A 690-pound bear was trapped in Yosemite in 1969. One reason why park bears are often heavy, according to Jane Tate, is that they supplement their diet with handouts from park visitors. Panhandling bears in Great Smoky Mountains National Park weigh more than those that do not panhandle.

Many people think black bears are even bigger than these weights indicate. When Michael Pelton, Gordon Burghardt, and Ronald Hietala, all of the University of Tennessee, took a survey of visitors' knowledge of black bears in Great Smoky Mountains National Park, some visitors said they thought black bears weighed 1000 to

2000 pounds! One reason people tend to overestimate the weight of black bears is that bears' long, dense fur makes their bodies appear to be bigger than they are. Another reason is that bears, unlike most other large wild animals, often rear up on their hind legs. Since we are not used to seeing animals on their hind legs, they look very large to us.

Bears are 4 to 6 feet (122 to 182 centimeters) long, on the average, so they are about that height when they rear up; a few rare ones reach 7 feet (213 centimeters). Standing on all fours, bears are about 2½ to 3 feet (76 to 91 centimeters) high.

One way to estimate the weight of a black bear is to look at the size and shape of its head, according to Albert Le Count, a wildlife biologist with the state of Arizona. All adult black bears have ears that are about 5 inches (13 centimeters) long, so if the ears are very noticeable, then the head is small and the bear is probably a small one. But if the ears are not prominent, the head is large and the bear is likely to be a big one. On a small bear, the ears also appear to be set close together, while on a large one, they are far apart, because the head is wide. Le Count adds that when viewed head on, a big bear's skull has a triangular shape, because of its width. A small bear's head is long, like that of most dogs.

Le Count has also worked out a method of estimating the size of black bears from their tracks, which is all that many people ever see of these secretive animals. If you find a front-foot track measuring more than 4¼ inches (11 centimeters) wide and long, including toes, it was probably made by an adult male. A hind-foot track at least 7½ inches (19 centimeters) long, includ-

A bear's weight can be estimated by the size and shape of its head. Ears of a small New York State bear (*left*) are closer together and more prominent than those of a larger Great Smoky Mountains National Park bear (*right*). (John O'Pezio, University of Tennessee)

ing toes, and 4 inches (10 centimeters) wide was also made by an adult male. If the front track is more than 5½ inches (14 centimeters) long or the hind track is more than 9 inches (23 centimeters) long, the bear that made them is an exceptionally large male.

The grizzly-brown and the polar, the other bears in North America, are much larger than the black bear. The brown bear weighs up to 1700 pounds (771 kilograms), which makes it the world's largest carnivore, or meat eater. The biggest grizzlies scale less than half as much as browns, at about 800 pounds (363 kilograms). The maximum weight for a polar bear is about 1500 pounds (680 kilograms).

No one has any trouble telling the polar from other bears, because of its distinctive white coloring, but confusion often arises over the grizzly and black bears. Some very large male black bears are the size of small female grizzlies and young male grizzlies, making it hard to distinguish the two species by size alone. The easiest way to tell these two animals apart, according to the Montana Department of Fish and Game, is the grizzly's hump, a raised area on the back between the shoulders. Another distinguishing feature, although not so dramatic as with the polar bear, is hair color. With few exceptions, black bears have black or brown hair, while most grizzlies have dark-brown hair with white tips, giving them the name "grizzly" or "silvertip."

Still another feature that helps in telling these two bears apart is their face. Most grizzlies have a concave nose-forehead area, while blacks have more of a straight-line profile.

For an animal of its size, the black bear is surprisingly fast. In 1961 two Wisconsin researchers driving a truck clocked a 200-pound (91-kilogram) black bear in Forest County at 33 miles (53 kilometers) an hour, a speed it kept up for the equivalent of a city block. Speeds of 30 miles an hour have been set by a number of other black bears. When a bear runs, its hind legs reach farther and farther forward and outward. This

This Wyoming black bear has the characteristic straight-line profile. Light-colored coat is typical of some Western bears. (U.S. Fish and Wildlife Service)

gait causes its back to hump up, so that the speeding animal resembles a ball, or, as the Wisconsin researchers put it, "an animated two-hundred-pound bowling ball."

Since the fastest a human can run is about 28 miles an hour, the average black bear can easily outdistance even the fastest person.

It doesn't do any good to climb a tree to get away from a black bear, either. Both adult and young black bears climb trees, although young animals do so more often. (Among grizzlies, on the other hand, only the young climb trees.) Black bears move fast up trees; one authority says they can climb almost as quickly as a squirrel. Going up, the bear clasps the tree with its front legs, while downward movements of the back legs propel it upward. Going down, it moves backward, like a cat, to a point where it can leap to the ground.

The black bear has special adaptations to help it climb. Compared with the grizzly, the claws of the black bear's front feet are shorter and more curved, to enable it to sink them into a tree. Another adaptation was pointed out recently by Ernest E. Reynolds, a California biology instructor. The bear penis is enclosed in a protective sheath similar to that of dogs. In black bears, an unusually long muscle connects the sheath to the front legs; when the animal climbs, the motion of the front legs pulls the sheath forward against the body and keeps the penis from being injured.

The general appearance of the black bear is that of a bulky, rounded animal with short, sturdy legs. A thick layer of fat under the skin and the dense, coarse hair are responsible for its round shape. The ears are small, as is the tail (about 5 inches — 13 centimeters) in

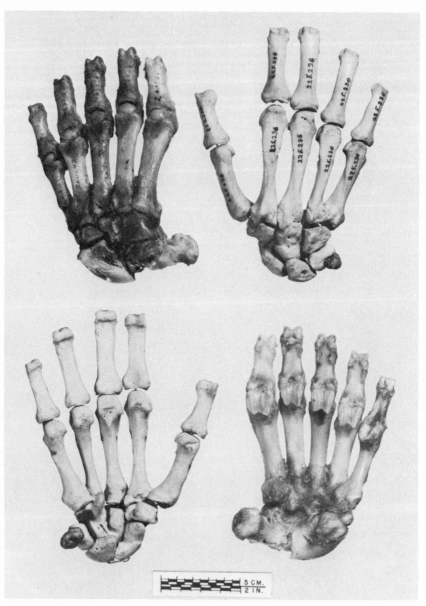

Skeletons of bear paws and human hands are surprisingly alike. Bear paws — upper left and lower right. (Smithsonian Institution and FBI Law Enforcement Bulletin)

adults. One of the most intriguing features of the black bear's anatomy is its feet, which are surprisingly human-looking. The front foot is round and shaped something like the human hand, while the hind foot is long and looks much like the human foot. Since bears walk on the soles of their feet, the way we do, the hind-foot track resembles that of a barefoot person. There are claws on all four feet. None can be retracted, or drawn back, like those of a cat.

When the claws and skin are missing from bear feet, the bones look even more like those of our own hands and feet. Every year, police departments around the United States get excited calls from people who think they have found the bones of human hands or feet. The bones usually turn out to be those of a black bear that was skinned for a hunting trophy. Some years ago, the *FBI Law Enforcement Bulletin* published an article by the anthropologist Dr. T. D. Stewart, of the Smithsonian Institution, advising police on how to distinguish bear paws from human hands and feet (see illustration, page 26).

As their name indicates, many black bears are black, but by no means are all black bears this color. They also come in brown, a steel-blue shade, and even white. And some black bears change color. Researchers such as Lynn Rogers, who have watched bears over long periods, have seen changes from black to brown and from brown to black. In most cases, these changes take place in yearling bears. Rogers found that female bears that had changed color were more likely to produce offspring that changed color, too.

In the eastern United States, black bears are usually

black, sometimes with a white patch on the chest. In the western United States, on the other hand, black bears are often brown. It's estimated that sixty per cent of the black bears in Arizona are really brown. Studies show that brown black bears are also common in the central Rocky Mountain region, in California, and in parts of the Pacific Northwest, including Canada. Minnesota has more brown black bears than any other region in the eastern half of the United States.

The blue black bear makes its home in a small area of southeastern Alaska and in Canada's Yukon Territory. Known as the "glacier bear," it is believed to inherit its unusual coloration from parents that carry the blue trait in their genes (genes are the basic unit of heredity). The blue trait seems to be recessive, which means it can be passed down to offspring only if both parents have the blue color gene. The San Diego Zoo now has the only glacier bear in captivity, Yakutat

The difference in color between a blue black, or "glacier," bear and the black phase of the same animal is apparent in this photograph taken at the San Diego Zoo. (San Diego Zoological Society)

Bluegenes. (San Diego Zoological Society)

Barry; the name comes from the area of Alaska where he was captured. Yakutat Barry recently acquired a black mate, Bluegenes, from the same area in Alaska. Bluegenes may carry the blue gene, as some black-colored bears in that area have it. If she does, some of the offspring she has with Yakutat Barry could be blue. As of this writing, the pair were still too young to mate.

The white black bear is found only on a few islands off British Columbia, in Canada, and it is rather rare even there. Actually, these bears are not white, like an albino (an animal that lacks pigmentation), but light tan; against the lush green forests of their home, the pale-tan fur looks white. Their eyes are a medium brown. (Other black bears have black eyes.) These white black bears are known as Kermode bears, for

Francis Kermode, the Canadian scientist who first described them in scientific terms.

No matter what color a black bear is, however, its muzzle, or snout, is always the same color: tan. This is another characteristic of black bears that helps distinguish them from grizzlies.

We don't know much about the senses of black bears, but recent research at the University of Tennessee sheds light on their vision. It demonstrates that black bears see color and shape. To test perception of color, Ellis Bacon gave two captive cubs, Kit and Kate, a board containing cups painted different colors. Each cup had a raisin under it but only one had a raisin the cubs could reach. For one cub, the right cup (the one with the raisin it could reach) was always blue, for the other, green. The position of the cups was changed to make sure the cubs were reacting to color, not position. The idea behind the experiment was for the cubs to look under the right cup first. Neither had any trouble figuring out which cup to look under first, even when the cups were painted in different shades of blue and green. The cubs did so well on this task, in fact, that Bacon believes black bears must use color vision in the wild to find small foods such as berries and nuts.

To test perception of shape, Bacon next gave one of the cubs, Kit, the same board and a number of small blocks with shapes painted on them. The shapes included circles, triangles, diamonds, and rectangles. The block with the triangle had a raisin the cub could reach under it. Kit had no trouble with this test, either, and her marks were just as high when the size and background of the shapes were changed. When Bacon tested Kit's memory for this task many months later, he found she remembered it very well.

The black bear's breeding biology has been deciphered by many researchers working in various areas of North America. Their observations show that maturity in black bears is not usually reached until about three and one-half years of age. This is the age at which most black bears mate for the first time. In some areas, however, black bears do not mate until they are four, five, or six years old — or even older. Most bears in Alaska delay maturity, studies show. On the other hand, bears in a few areas of the United States seem to mature as early as two and one-half. The reason for delayed maturity in bears is not clear, but it probably has something to do with scarcity of food: in northern climates, where the delay has been noticed, the growing season is short and there is less food available.

Mating in black bears most often takes place in June and July. The female gives birth some seven months later, when she is hibernating in her den.

Until shortly before the young appear, the female shows no signs of pregnancy. This is because of an unusual phenomenon called delayed implantation. In most other mammals, an egg fertilized by male sperm attaches itself to the wall of the female's uterus soon after mating. There it grows steadily until birth. In black bears, however, the fertilized egg, having developed into a tiny ball, simply floats in the fluid within the uterus. Only when the mother is hibernating in her den does the fetus attach itself to the wall of the uterus and begin again to grow. Because of this process, the total time for growth in the black-bear fetus is only forty-two to fifty-six days, even though pregnancy is seven months long. This kind of reproduction, which is also found in other bears and some other mammals, probably occurs in order to allow the female to build up her bodily reserves in late summer and early fall, when food is abundant. Bears put on most of their weight in this period in preparation for hibernation.

Researchers who study animals with delayed implantation have speculated for many years about the factors that affect the process. What triggers the fetus's second and final period of growth? Although no clear answers have been found, it seems likely that the lengthening days of midwinter have something to do with it. In the marten, another animal with delayed implantation, the length of pregnancy in captive animals can be shortened significantly by increasing the length of the day artificially. No one has done this with bears, but the same response to light may occur in all animals with delayed implantation.

The black bear's litter normally consists of one, two, or three cubs. Four is unusual and five extremely unusual; there are a handful of cases on record of six cubs. The newborn young weigh only about a half-pound (227 grams) apiece, a very small size for the large animals they will become. They are about 8 inches (20 centimeters) long. Not only are the newborn cubs tiny, but they are also blind, and have so little hair they appear naked. But they grow rapidly and by the time they leave the den, in April or May, they weigh about 5 pounds (2.3 kilograms) and have a thick coat of hair.

Females normally give birth every other year, a schedule dictated by the cycle of the mother's body.

During the first year after bearing young, the mother is lactating, producing milk for her cubs. Lactation prevents the mother from going into the fertile period, called estrus, which leads to mating. The following year, when the cubs are a year and a half old, the mother goes into estrus and mates. This schedule can be upset if the young are removed from the mother when they are still nursing. If that happens, the mother goes into estrus, mates, and bears young just a year after her last litter.

Captive female bears in a study in North Carolina produced cubs every year for a number of years. In each case, their cubs were removed when they were just a few months old.

Old age doesn't seem to interfere with black-bear reproduction. Lynn Rogers found a twenty-year-old female, which is very old for a bear in the wild, with two young cubs. A captive bear in a zoo produced her last litter at the age of twenty-four.

Animals that take a long time to mature and carry their young within their bodies for a long time usually have the capacity for a long life. The black bear is no exception. In 1974, a hunter shot a male in New York State that was forty-one years old (as determined by the cementum-annuli technique). It is the oldest black bear known. Another bear killed in New York was found to be thirty-four and three-quarters. Other black bears in their thirties have been found and almost every survey of a large bear population turns up a few animals in their twenties.

Although the oldest black bear was a male, most long-lived bears are females. This is because males cover much more ground in their movements, making them more likely to be killed at a young age by hunters and farmers and in road accidents. Even where bears are not hunted, females tend to outlive males. In Great Smoky Mountains National Park, for instance, the average age of the female bears is six and three-quarters years, the average age of the males four and a half years. The oldest female ever captured in the park was about fifteen years old. The oldest male was about twelve.

One factor that is associated with the relatively long life of black bears is their healthiness. On the whole, studies of black bears find few signs of disease or other unhealthy conditions in the animals. They do, however, have worms similar to those found in domestic dogs and other mammals. The larvae of one of these worms can produce the disease trichinosis in humans if they eat meat from an infected bear without cooking it properly. Black bears can also get leptospirosis, a serious infectious disease common in dogs.

Since black bears are healthy and capable of long lives, there might soon be too many of them in some areas if other factors did not keep the population down. One of these factors is man. Bears are a game animal in most states today, so hunting removes many of them from areas outside protected parks. The killing of problem animals that raid crops and get into other trouble also holds down the number of bears.

Moreover, bears have their own way of controlling their population. Lynn Rogers, who studied black bears over a period of nine years in Minnesota, found that during one three-year period of scarce food, the interval between litters became as long as four years, instead of the normal two; one bear in the study did not have cubs until she was seven years old. Furthermore, half of the cubs that were born during this period and three-fourths of the yearlings died. Many of them starved.

How many black bears are there in the United States today? Probably between 175,000 and 225,000, most of them in the western United States. Alaska undoubtedly has the greatest number, some 40,000 to 50,000. Next comes Idaho, with about 40,000; Washington, with 27,000 to 30,000; Oregon, with 20,000 to 25,000; California, with 11,000 to 15,000; and Montana, with 8,000 to 10,000. Colorado has about 7,000. In the eastern half of the country, Maine has the most black bears, 7,000 to 10,000, but Wisconsin is close behind, with 6,000 to 8,000. Michigan has 5,000 to 6,000, New York about 4,000.

The density of black bears — the number of animals in a particular geographic area — varies widely. The highest known density in the United States occurs in Great Smoky Mountains National Park. Parts of the park have one bear for every .3 square mile (.89 square kilometer). A section of Trinity County, California, has one bear for every .5 square mile (1.3 square kilometer). In large areas of the Alaskan wilderness, on the other hand, there are fewer than one bear per 100 square miles (260 square kilometers). Some other densities are one bear per 6 square miles (14.3 square kilometers) in Maine, one bear per 4 square miles (10.1 square kilometers) in Virginia, one per 2 square miles (4.7 square kilometers) in Minnesota, and more than one bear per square mile (2.6 square kilometers) in Washington.

The only other countries in which American black

bears live are Mexico and Canada. In Mexico, the southern limit of their range, there are probably only a small number of black bears (they live in northern Mexico), but in Canada the animals are more plentiful than they are in the United States. Every Canadian province and territory has black bears. Some recent population estimates are: Newfoundland, 100,000; British Columbia, 75,000 or more, and Saskatchewan, 25,000 or more. Other provinces and territories probably have as many or more black bears.

All these figures are estimates. We don't know exactly how many black bears there are, or how dense their population is, because no completely reliable way of counting them has yet been developed. One way in which wildlife biologists estimate bear populations is by capturing a number of animals in an area, marking them with a tag or tattoo, and releasing them. Then as many bears as possible are captured in the same area. The proportion, or ratio, of marked to unmarked bears in the second round of captures should be about the same as the ratio of marked bears to the whole population. This formula is called the Lincoln index.

Michael Pelton, of the University of Tennessee, has developed a promising new way to count bears using the Lincoln index and its modifications. He and his students capture bears in Great Smoky Mountains National Park and inject them with small amounts of a radioactive material (it does not harm the animals). After the bears are released, the students hike the trails in the park and collect bear scat, the dry, solid excrement of the animals. If the bears have been injected with the radioactive material, the scats reveal it under laboratory tests. The number of radioactive scats is totaled and that figure is used in the Lincoln index in the same way as the total number of recaptured marked bears.

The advantage of collecting scats instead of recapturing bears, according to Pelton, is that scats can be gathered from more of the bears in an area, making the population estimate more accurate. With the old recapture technique, some marked bears become frightened of the researchers and avoid being caught again. In addition, scats are collected over a whole summer, so there are a number of ratios that can be averaged, not just one. This adds to the accuracy of the method, too.

CHAPTER III

"A Great Blacke Kind of Beare"

The black-bear story begins about twenty-five million years ago, in the Miocene epoch. At that time, bears split off from the group of animals that later became the canids (dogs, wolves, coyotes, foxes). Bears and hyenas are the most recent members of the canids to strike out on their own, and bears still have some canid characteristics. One is the way they play. A young bear, for instance, will often grab the muzzle of another young bear in its mouth and squeeze gently, much the way wolves and coyotes do. J. D. Henry and Dr. Stephen M. Herrero, of the University of Calgary, Canada, who have compared canid and bear play, believe their work proves the close relationship that once existed between bears and canids.

Although one authority puts canids and bears in the same scientific family, most other experts give bears a separate family, the ursines. The Latin name is Ursidae.

The first ursine, or bear, for which we have a fossil record appeared about five million years ago, in Europe. Called the Auvergne bear, the species looked like a small version of the modern black bear. The ancient Auvergne bear probably lived in the forests that covered much of Europe at that time. Between one and three million years ago, this bear evolved into another forest-living bear, the Etruscan bear. The most recent forms of this species were as large as today's brown bears.

While the Etruscan bear was roaming the forests of Europe, enormous changes were taking place in the earth's climate and geology. The Pleistocene epoch, or the Ice Age, was coming. The changes it brought led, over the centuries, to great migrations on the part of many species, including bears. Sometime in the Ice Age, the Etruscan bear traveled from Europe to Asia. From there, it made another centuries-long move, this time over a land bridge that had formed between Asia and North America, at Alaska. The bear's movement over the bridge took place sometime earlier than 500,000 B.P. (Before Present). We know this because bones of the Asiatic bear dating from about 500,000 B.P. have been found in a cave in Pennsylvania.

This carving of a black bear's head comes from a house used by a Northwest Coast Indian tribe. The teeth are made from mollusk shell. (American Museum of Natural History)

These early bears became the ancestors of today's black bears. For hundreds of thousands of years, they were the only bears in North America. The brown and grizzly bears also descended from the same small Asiatic bear, but they postponed their journey over the Asiatic land bridge to sometime after 100,000 B.P. Once they arrived in North America, the grizzlies may have been confined to Alaska by the glaciers of the Ice Age, which prevented them from traveling south until most of the ice had melted. The polar bears probably evolved from brown bears that lived beside the sea in North America.

Experts put browns and grizzlies in the same species today. Polar bears and black bears belong to different species.

There is a modern Asiatic black bear, *Selenarctos*, living in southern and eastern Asia, but it is no longer closely related to any of the North American bears.

The black, grizzly-brown, and polar bears are the only bears in North America. Most grizzlies (subspecies *horribilis*) are now found in Alaska and parts of western Canada, although there are a few in the northwestern United States; they once ranged throughout the western United States and into Mexico. Polar bears live all around the Arctic Circle, including the extreme northern edge of our continent. The huge brown bears (subspecies *middendorfi*), the world's largest meat-eating animal, live only in Alaska in this hemisphere, but they also inhabit parts of Europe and Asia.

Before the Europeans settled in what later became the United States, there were black bears almost everywhere in North America. Of the three bears in North America, the polar, grizzly-brown and black, the last

had by far the widest range and largest numbers. Its range extended from northern Mexico through Canada, and from the Atlantic to the Pacific. It was the only bear east of the Mississippi. The black bear was scarce in the few parts of the West that lacked suitable habitat, but in most places in the country it was hard *not* to see one. In 1688 a Jesuit missionary, Father Jacques Gravier, saw fifty black bears in a single day near the mouth of the Ohio River.

How many black bears were there before the whites came? It's impossible to say, but experts estimate there were at least 500,000, and perhaps as many as a million or more.

For a long time before the Europeans arrived, the plentiful black bear shared its territory with the American Indian. To the many tribes east of the Mississippi, it was the only bear known. Archaeologists have found the bones of black bears at Indian sites in the East that are many thousands of years old.

The Indians held bears in high regard. One of the most common Indian beliefs about bears was that they were able to cure disease. The Pueblos of the Southwest thought disease was caused by witches and that the bear, being a big, strong animal, could fight these witches. When a medicine man was called on to help cure a patient, he would wear something connected with bears, such as a pair of hairy bearskin gloves, and possibly dance around imitating a bear. Some Pueblos and California Indians claimed medicine men could change themselves into bears and went to a kind of bear heaven when they died, instead of the heaven reserved for most people.

Among other tribes, medicine men were believed to

have acquired their powers to cure disease by dreaming of a bear: the animal told them where to find curative herbs and roots, and gave other information on treating illness. (One reason bears were thought to know so much about curing was that they were often seen eating the plants used as herbs by the Indians.) Medicine men in these tribes wore items related to bears when they practiced their art. Some chewed "bear's root," or aster root, to enable them to "see" the cause of the illness.

Another common Indian belief about bears was that they are somewhat human — possibly even godlike. It's easy to see why Indians thought this. Bears sometimes stand on two legs, just like people, and some of their bones look very much like those of humans. Then, too, bears seem to like the same foods as man, and they sometimes kill other animals for food, just as man does. Among one group of Pueblo, the Isleta, the belief in the humanity of bears was so strong that they never killed the animal. "Bear is a person, men would not kill one," an Isletan told an anthropologist.

The Isletan attitude toward bears is unusual, but all the Pueblos thought the bear was much more than an animal. The hunter who killed one, for instance, was eligible to join a warriors' society, just as if he had killed a man; the bear's skin had the same value as an enemy's scalp. Pueblos believed bears had supernatural powers, too. Bears were associated with the two great Pueblo deities, the Spirit of the West and the Mother of Game, the latter the goddess of the game animals. In dances, the impersonator of the Mother of Game sometimes wore a bear disguise.

The Cherokees, a large Indian tribe living in the

Cherokee black bear mask from the Qualla Reservation in North Carolina was worn by hunters in a dance requesting good luck. (Museum of the American Indian — Heye Foundation)

southeastern United States, put bears in a special category. To the Cherokees, the bear represented the division between people and animals, and bears were descended from people. Long ago, according to a Cherokee legend, all the Cherokees in a certain town decided to live in the forest with the animals, so that they would always have enough to eat. Other Cherokees sent messengers to the forest to try to persuade them to come back, but when the messengers arrived they saw that the people already had long black hair like bears. The bear-people refused to return.

"Hereafter we shall be called bears and when you yourselves are hungry, come into the woods and call us and we shall come to give you our own flesh," one of the bear-people said. "You need not be afraid to kill us, for we shall live always."

As the messengers were leaving they looked back, and saw a group of black bears going into the forest.

This legend illustrates the Cherokees' belief that a bear did not really die when it was apparently killed. It simply returned to its hidden home in the forest or swamp, and resumed its life. This belief, which was shared by most North American Indians, explains how these people were able to kill an animal they regarded as almost human or godlike. Nevertheless, holding this animal in such high regard required that the hunting of it and other actions connected with its death be carried out in a certain way. If these rules were not followed, the bear's ghost would take revenge on the killer.

The rules cover many aspects of the bear hunt and the feast that followed. Before going on a hunt, the hunter equipped himself with various charms designed both to attract bears and to pacify their spirit when they were killed. The American Museum of Natural History displays an unusual charm made from the skins of the chins of black bears: tied into the bundle of skins are small bones from bears, each bone encased in a little leather packet. Another charm in the same collection is made from bear claws, and another from a bear's shoulder blade, painted red. All these charms were used by Eastern Woodland Indians, who were familiar with only one bear, the black.

Bears were hunted by Indians in a number of ways. They could be shot with a bow and arrow, clubbed, speared, or killed in traps. In one kind of Indian trap used all over the country, the deadfall, a large log fell on the bear as it tried to get food. Where large trees were scarce, bears might be captured in a pitfall trap, which is a concealed pit dug in the earth.

In the eastern United States the favored way of hunting a black bear was to drive it out of hibernation by tossing some flaming material into its winter den. Before the bear emerged, the hunters would call to it:

"Come out, Grandfather! We don't want to hurt you." When the sleepy animal appeared, the hunters attacked it with spears or arrows, apologizing as they killed it.

The skinning, butchering, distribution, and eating of bear meat were also usually subject to rules. In some tribes, the first portions went to the older men or other important figures. Women were allowed to eat only certain parts.

The tribes that lived around the Great Lakes had particularly elaborate ceremonies connected with butchering and eating a bear. The head was removed and decorated with beadwork and ribbons, and the hide was laid out on a mat. Then the body was carefully disjointed with a knife. Meanwhile, invitations were sent to neighboring villages to participate in the bear feast. At the feast, favorite foods of bears were displayed, along with a man's or woman's outfit, depending on the bear's sex. While the rest of the group ate the bear meat, one Indian addressed the bears back in their "village." He pointed out how well the present bear was being treated and promised similar treatment for other bears.

The Pueblo rites surrounding the bear hunt were equally complex. After killing a bear, the hunter alerted his village and everyone trooped out to the death scene. Each person made a mock attack on the dead bear, either "striking" or "shooting" it. Then the group carried the carcass back to the village while singing. To the Pueblo Indians, the bear meat had no special significance, but the rest of the body received careful attention. The paws went to the medicine man, the skull was buried, and the bones were placed in

shrines or in the river. The skin, which had the sym-
bolic value of a human scalp, was carried around the
village by chanting tribesmen.

Indians put the body of the black bear to many prac-
tical uses. Bear was one of the Indians' favorite meats.
A popular dish of the Southeastern Indians was a soup
made of black-bear meat, squash, and kernels of corn
all boiled together in a pot. Another way the Indians
cooked bear was to cut it into chunks and barbecue it
on sticks or spits. The bearskin was turned into blankets and clothing, the intestines were twisted into bow-
strings, and the teeth and claws were made into
charms. The paws, as mentioned, were reserved for
gloves worn by medicine men.

The most versatile bear product was bear oil. Bears
carry a thick layer of fat under their skin, and when the
fat is cooked, it yields a large quantity of light-colored
oil. Many Indian tribes seem to have killed bears principally for the fat, not the meat, because the oil was
employed in so many ways. Indians cooked food in
bear oil, dabbed it on certain foods as a kind of mayon-
naise, rubbed sore muscles with it, coated their hair
with it, and used it as a baby oil, among many other
applications. The early white explorers and trappers,
who learned about bear oil from the Indians, also
found numerous uses for it. Some of the French trappers even claimed it was superior to olive oil in cooking!

Although the black bear was put to so many uses by
the Indians, they did not kill an excessive number of
bears. The Indians practiced an effective kind of conservation with all animals. Many tribes had hunting
seasons, restricted the number of animals that could be

killed, and hunted only in areas where the animal's population was large enough not to be depleted by hunting. "No Indian will kill a bear in the season for hunting deer," reported one early European writer. The attitude of the Cherokees toward game is illustrated in one of their legends. All the animals got together and complained that the human population was becoming too large and killing too many animals. Even worse, the hunters were not asking the animals' pardon before killing them. In revenge, the animals gave man disease. As anthropologist Charles Hudson, of the University of Tennessee, points out, this legend shows that the Cherokees realized they had to practice care in exploiting Nature, or it would strike back.

The Indians' conservation practices, and the fact that their agriculture had little effect on the land, allowed both the black and the grizzly bears to thrive in the area that later became the United States. When the white colonists arrived in the sixteenth century, the black bear was very common along the Eastern Seaboard, the first area settled. Until the West was opened, it was the only American bear known to the settlers. Accounts from Colonial days often mention the black bear. "Beares they be common, being a great blacke kind of Beare . . . ," wrote William Wood, an Englishman, in 1634 about the newly settled area near modern Boston.

North of Massachusetts, in what later became New Hampshire, bears were, if anything, even more in evidence. Early in the seventeenth century, the settlers at Dover hired Indians to kill bears that were menacing their livestock. Colonists in the South, too, had numerous bears to contend with. Gabriel Arthur, who explored the mountains of western North Carolina from 1670 to 1680, found "beare" to be one of the most common animals. A few decades later, naturalist John Lawson reported that the black bear was common in coastal South Carolina. When naturalists John and William Bartram explored the wilderness that was Florida in the 1770s, they saw eleven bears in one day.

Surrounded by black bears, the white settlers quickly developed a number of uses for them. "It is wholesome and nourishing and resembles pork more than any other meat," runs an enthusiastic eighteenth-century note on black-bear meat. In Massachusetts, bear meat was available on the market, where it sold for up to twopence a pound from 1721 to 1759. The skins proved even more popular. From the early seventeenth to the late nineteenth century — almost three hundred years — bearskins were a common item in the fur trade. Ernest Thompson Seton, the naturalist, found documents that show fur companies sold some 18,000 bearskins a year in the early part of this period. At that time, a bearskin sold in New England for about forty silver shillings, a very substantial sum. Today, bearskins may not be sold in most states, but in Canada, where it is legal to sell them, prices in recent years have run as high as seventy-five dollars apiece.

Bearskins were popular because they are heavy and durable, qualities that made them desirable for use as rugs, blankets, muffs, and even overcoats. These items held up for many years. When Ben East, the writer, was a child in the early twentieth century, his father wore a bearskin coat inherited from East's grandfather. As young East and his mother shivered in the

Nineteenth-century bear-oil bottle. (Museum of the Fur Trade, Chadron, Nebraska)

family's open sleigh, the father kept warm in the heavy coat.

Bear oil found almost as many uses among the settlers as it did among the Indians, and some uses to which the Indians never put it. The Indians seldom ate uncooked greens as salads, but the settlers did, and they discovered bear oil made a good salad oil. They also used it as a hair "restorer," a practice mentioned as early as 1682. The demand for bear-oil hair restorer, in fact, continued right up to the end of the nineteenth century; in 1872 a hunter in Wisconsin killed a black bear that yielded "ten gallons of hair oil." (A black bear usually gives from 10 to 15 gallons — 38 to 57 liters — of oil.) The early settlers also used bear oil, as mentioned, for cooking, as a liniment ("very efficacious in rheumatic complaints," says a 1784 account), and in perfume.

But in spite of all the uses found for black bears, the animal and the white settlers were soon engaged in a war that ended only with the bear being reduced to a remnant of its original population, particularly in the East. The conflict was probably inevitable. The black bear is a creature of forests and swamps. On occasion it eats meat, but most of its diet is vegetable matter. The settlers cut down most of the forest and drained some of the swamps to make farms. Then they grew things on the farms that bears like to eat, especially corn. Bear problems began as soon as the settlers arrived. The animals wandered through farms and even towns, eating corn and other crops, and sometimes killing a pig, lamb, or calf. On rare occasions, they caused an injury or death to a pursuing settler.

Bear damage seems to have been exceptionally severe in New Hampshire. An eighteenth-century historian of that state wrote about bears:

In the months of August and September, he makes great havoc in the fields of Indian corn, in the new settlements. He places himself between two rows of corn, and with his paws breaks down the stalks of four contiguous hills, bending them toward the center of the space, that the ears may lie near to each other, and then devours them. Passing in this manner through the field, he destroys the corn in great quantities.

In most other areas, according to written accounts, black-bear damage was not severe, though it was enough to give settlers what now seems like an unreasonable hatred of bears. Bears came to be regarded as vermin, noxious creatures to be killed on sight. This attitude was given legal status in the bounty system.

A bounty is a payment made on the presentation of the body, or some other evidence of death, of a designated species of animal. Bears were bountied early in Colonial times. In 1666 the town of Fairfield, Connecticut, set a one-year bounty of fifty shillings for adult bears and twenty shillings for cubs. Springfield, Massachusetts, in 1686 set a bounty of four shillings for

Nineteenth-century Canadian fur buyers examining skins collected by Indians. (Provincial Archives of Alberta)

adults and two shillings for cubs. In 1695 South Carolina passed an "Act for Destroying Beasts of Prey" which *required* every Indian warrior to turn in each year either two bobcat skins or the pelt of a wolf, panther, or bear. The alternative: a whipping.

Bounties continued well into the twentieth century in many areas, even though bear damage was no longer a problem. New Hampshire paid 1165 bear bounties from 1951 through 1955. A few counties in Virginia still have bear bounties on the books.

Bounties, plus the additional money that could be made by selling a bearskin to a fur dealer, encouraged the large-scale killing of black bears that occurred all over the United States for two hundred and fifty years. Unlike the pre-Colonial Indians, the white settlers and their descendants often hunted with dogs, which proved to be the most effective way to kill bears. A dog can "tree" a bear — force it to climb a tree — and then the bear can be easily killed with a gun. Bear trapping was also widely practiced, the deadfall being replaced by a heavy steel trap with sharp spikes. Dogs, guns, and steel traps soon resulted in high bear kills. Moses Leonard, who lived in Greenfield, Massachusetts, in the second half of the eighteenth century, claimed a lifetime score of 150 black bears. In 1714, 500 bears were killed over one winter in two counties in Virginia. Four Wisconsin men killed twelve bears in seven days in 1874, taking six of the animals within five minutes.

Mountainous West Virginia apparently had an unusually high number of bears. In three years early in the nineteenth century, hunters took 8000 bearskins in one small area there. Another limited area yielded a hunter thirteen bears in an afternoon.

Even the Indians, traditionally conservationists, got in on the bear overkill. Fifty-four Wisconsin Indians killed almost a thousand bears in the fall and winter of 1827–28. There is ample evidence that Northeastern tribes in Canada and the United States — who had once regarded the bear as almost sacred — supplied fur traders with large numbers of bearskins. Why did the Indians change their traditional view of the bear? Most historians believe the Indians simply desired the white man's goods, which they could obtain in exchange for furs. But another historian, Dr. Calvin Martin of Rutgers University, believes Indians turned to the excessive slaughtering of animals because they blamed the animals for the epidemic diseases that killed large numbers of Indians after their first contacts with the Europeans. At the turn of the nineteenth century, Dr. Martin points out, Cree and Ojibway tribes in the upper Great Lakes region spoke of a conspiracy of animals against mankind, for which the animals had to be destroyed. In actuality, of course, it was not the animals but the Europeans who transmitted these epidemic diseases.

In the last part of the nineteenth century a new factor began affecting black bears: large-scale logging. There had always been logging in the United States, but during this period logging operations became more extensive, reaching farther into remote areas — the very areas where black bears had retreated under the earlier pressures of farming and bounty hunting. In the Great Smoky Mountains of Tennessee and North Carolina, once the home of the Cherokee Indians (there is still a large Cherokee reservation there), logging begun about 1900 was extending up to 4000 feet above sea level. The lower slopes had once been full of bears, but after this time bears were seldom seen there.

It was the same in the Mississippi lowlands. William Faulkner wrote a famous story, "The Bear," about a boy hunting a black bear in this part of Mississippi. Shortly after the period portrayed in the story, lumber companies cut down most of the lowland timber. Now there are farms in the lowlands, but bears, if any, are rare.

Mississippi isn't the only state where black bears are rare today. By the opening of the twentieth century, the combination of bounty hunting and forest clearing for farming and logging had reduced black-bear populations all over the country. The states that lost the most bears were those that lost the most forest and swampland. In these states, the black bear had no place to hide. New Jersey, southern New England, most of the Southern and Midwestern states, the Dakotas, and Oklahoma saw the disappearance of most of their black bears. Many of these states have no black bears now, although the animal once roamed there in large numbers. Fur trader Alexander Henry's journal of his experiences in North Dakota in the early 1800s reports that his trappers collected 746 black-bear skins from 1800 through 1805; today there are no black bears in the Dakotas.

The story of the black bear's decline and eventual disappearance in my home state of Missouri is a typical one. Missouri has a long history, having been settled by French fur trappers and traders in the early eighteenth century. At that time, black bears were very common. The French were more interested in the skins of other animals, but early records indicate that these first Missouri settlers did eat the meat of bears. By the early nineteenth century, bearskins had become a fairly valuable item of commerce in Missouri. Moses Austin's store in Ste. Genevieve, on the Mississippi River, had records of more than 100 bearskins that were either brought into the store or shipped to New York from 1806 though 1811; one lot was worth $1.25 apiece, about the same as beaver.

The Lewis and Clark Expedition was in Missouri for about two months in 1804, during which time the men shot ten to fourteen black bears for food. By then, bears were not so common as they had been the century before; the expedition did not see a bear until it had gone halfway across the state via the Missouri River. In 1823 Paul Wilhelm, a German traveler, journeyed up the Missouri River and was attacked on shore by a black bear; he shot the animal. Wilhelm saw at least three more bears, but he remarked that bears were few in eastern Missouri, an impression confirmed by one of his companions, a Missouri-born hunter.

But in other areas of Missouri bears were still plentiful. One Missouri Valley resident, who made his living by hunting, claimed to have killed fifty bears in the autumn of 1818. Another Missouri Valley resident remembered killing as many as two or three bears a day about 1820. Large numbers of bears were being taken by hunters in the 1830s in New Madrid County, in southeastern Missouri; swampy parts of this region still had many bears in the 1880s. Henry Rowe Schoolcraft, a traveler, made numerous references to bears in his notes on the Ozark Mountains in south-central and south-western Missouri in the winter of 1818–19.

By the middle of the nineteenth century, the black

Bears were considered both frightening and funny, as this 1866 print shows. From *100 Currier and Ives Favorites*, Albert K. Baragwanath. (Crown Publishers and Harry T. Peters Collection, Museum of the City of New York)

bear was gone from the Missouri Valley, which had become a well-populated farming region. The last bear, weighing 400 pounds (180 kilograms), was shot by a party of hunters in 1859 in Moniteau County, in the center of the state. Black bears lingered on in the heavily wooded Ozarks until the late nineteenth century, and in remote swamps in southeastern Missouri until well into the twentieth century. These were the parts of the state "uncongenial and relatively worthless to man," as Daniel McKinley, of Ohio's Lake Erie College, puts it in his history of the black bear in Missouri. The last record for a native Missouri black bear dates from 1931, in the southeastern part of the state. There were no black bears in Missouri for several decades but recently some wandered into the state from neighbor-

California hunter lassoes a black bear in this nineteenth-century engraving. (New York Public Library Picture Collection)

ing Arkansas, which has been restocking bears. A small breeding population now lives in the southern part of the Missouri Ozarks.

In other places, however, the picture was brighter for the black bear, even at the height of the bounty-hunting fever. Maine, New York, Michigan, Wisconsin, Colorado, Idaho, Montana, California, Oregon, Washington, and Alaska all retained large tracts of wooded, mountainous land, which provided a refuge for many black bears. They are still numerous in all these states, although the animals are now restricted to the wilder areas.

Toward the end of the nineteenth century, a new interest in conservation resulted in the opening of the first national parks, in the Western states. Hunting and trapping are not permitted in national parks, which gives the black bear complete protection in these areas. Later, the creation of wildlife refuges and national forests in the West provided additional protection, although hunting there is permitted.

Black bears also managed to hang on, in small numbers, in parts of the Southeast. Some of the last bear retreats — mountains and swamps — eventually became national and state parks, wildlife refuges, and national forests, and here is where most of the Southeastern bears now live. In a few cases, the protection afforded by these areas has enabled the bears to increase their numbers. When Great Smoky Mountains National Park was opened, in 1934, bears in the area had dwindled to between 50 and 200, owing to logging, agriculture, and excessive hunting. But within just a few years, bears began to appear in places within the park where they had not been seen for many years. By 1941 their population was estimated at 400; now it may be between 500 and 600. A park visitor today has as good a chance of seeing a black bear as a Cherokee Indian did in the seventeenth century. In fact, the visitor's chances may be better, as a few park bears have learned to beg from tourists and make regular appearances along the park's roads.

Wildlife experts believe that the late 1800s may have marked the low point for black bears in this country. After that time, several trends began to work in the bears' favor. One was the new system of parks, wildlife refuges, and national forests. Another was the reversion of some former farmland to woodland, particularly in the Northeast. In the forty years between 1880 and 1920, the area of improved farmland in the North-

State game wardens enforce bear hunting regulations. Richard Perry of Virginia with a bear cub. (Virginia Commission of Game and Inland Fisheries)

east dropped thirty per cent. The new woodlands were most noticeable in southern New England, most of which had been covered with small farms since the eighteenth century. Although some of the oaks and chestnuts that have grown up on the old farms are now felled for lumber, New England's forests are growing faster than they are being cut.

Soon after the onset of forest regrowth, reports of bears began coming in from western Connecticut, western Massachusetts, and southern New Hampshire, areas where bears had not been seen since the mid-nineteenth century. Bears also started trickling back to former agricultural land in New York and Pennsylvania.

A third trend that helped black bears was their designation as a game animal. The movement toward game status began early in the twentieth century, but many states did not join it until midcentury. Now black bears — when not completely protected — are classified as game in almost all states with a bear population. It may seem strange that the status of game animal confers a benefit on a species, but before the black bear gained this status, it had been a bountied animal in most states — that meant it could be killed anywhere, any time, and in any number. By making the bear a game animal, state wildlife officials were able to impose a bear-hunting season and limit the number of bears that could be killed. Moreover, most states have made certain ways of killing bears illegal. In the eastern half of the country, some states with very small bear populations — including Connecticut and Alabama — have given complete protection to the bear. Here bears may not be killed unless they cause severe damage to property or menace human beings.

In some states, ingenious measures have been taken to preserve the black bear. Between 1959 and 1968 Arkansas imported about 300 black bears from Minnesota and Canada. At the time the transplant was begun, Arkansas had only 50 bears; now it has 1200 to 1500, according to Bobby W. Conley, of the Arkansas Game and Fish Commission. The majority live in Ozark National Forest. Louisiana transplanted 161 black bears from Minnesota between 1964 and 1967. Most were females with cubs. In 1971 David F. Taylor, of the Louisiana Department of Wildlife and Fisheries, surveyed the Atchafalaya basin, near Lottie, Louisiana, where most of the bears had been released, and he found many signs of the animals there.

CHAPTER IV

A Black Bear's Biography

For a black bear, life starts in its mother's den in December, January, or February. The mother is hibernating, and she may not even be aware of the cubs' birth, according to some researchers. The newborn cubs, blind and weighing only about a half pound (227 grams) apiece, crawl to their mother's nipples and nurse. In her sleep she curls herself around them to keep them warm.

One of the few people to observe a newborn black bear in the wild is Harold O. Guiher, of Sabula, Pennsylvania. In December 1951 Guiher was hunting deer in Clearfield County, Pennsylvania, when he came across a female bear in a hole under a log. Guiher visited the den frequently after that, and on January 4 he heard the squeaks of several cubs. When he saw two cubs a few days later, they looked like "little tan-colored pigs about the size of a rat."

By mid-January, the cubs looked to Guiher more like little dogs. They had smooth brown fur and pink feet, much like the feet of a human baby. Their eyes were closed, and Guiher did not see them open until February 12. Their fur got progressively darker as the weeks passed, and by March 8 it was quite black. When Guiher saw the family outside the den in late March,

This bear cub being raised by New York State researchers was about five weeks old when this photograph was taken. (John O'Pezio, New York State Department of Environmental Conservation)

he was surprised to find the mother had three cubs, not two. At this time, when the cubs were about two and a half months old, they climbed a tree to a height of about two feet.

Stephen M. Herrero, of the University of Calgary — whose work is mentioned in Chapter III — made some observations of a black-bear cub in the wild for about a month. He had been watching an occupied bear den in Banff National Park, in Alberta, and on a warm day in late February he saw a female bear come out. She went back in and came out again, this time carrying a single young cub by the skin on top of its head. She put it down on the snow-free ground and scraped up some leaves and other forest debris into a pile. Then she put the cub on the pile.

Herrero judged the cub's age to be about forty days, since bear cubs are born in December and January in that area. Its eyes were just beginning to open and it was covered with thick black hair. The animal was about 16 inches (41 centimeters) long.

When Herrero first saw the cub, it was unable to walk at all, but about a week later it suddenly struggled to its feet and took two shaky steps. Then it fell on its little snout. That same day, it succeeded in walking in a circle several feet in diameter. The cub's progress after that was rapid — within a month it was not only walking but also climbing trees. By then it was about two and a half months old, the same age as the cubs Guiher saw climbing trees.

A few years ago New York State's Big Game Unit got an even closer look at three very young black-bear cubs. The animals, estimated to be two weeks old, were turned over to the Unit at Delmar (near Albany) after having been found abandoned by their mother. She had probably been frightened from the den by hunters; occasionally, when disturbed, bear mothers will abandon their young. The cubs weighed less than 2 pounds (.9 kilogram) apiece and had a thin covering of black hair. Their eyes were closed but they already had sharp teeth — the biologists and technicians in the Unit wore heavy gloves to handle the tiny bears. Milk in baby bottles was given to them every hour. Most of the time they squalled.

Work in the Big Game Unit was becoming difficult under these conditions, so the offer of another New York State employee to care for the cubs was quickly accepted. Meanwhile, the Unit pondered the young bears' future: How could they return to the wild without a mother to teach them how to survive? At that time, the Unit had four radio-collared adult female bears in the northern Catskill Mountains. All were in their dens, since it was mid-February. A plan was decided on. If one of the females had cubs, the abandoned cubs would be placed with her in hopes that she would accept them as her own when she awakened in the spring. No one had ever made a foster mother out of a black bear before, so it was not known how the female would react. But the Unit believed it was worth taking a chance.

The openings of all the dens were too small to see what was inside, but the researchers pushed microphones in and recorded sounds. From one den came the unmistakable squalling of cubs (only too familiar to the Unit by now). The volume of noise attested to at least one cub, and possibly two.

Since the mother was believed to have several cubs

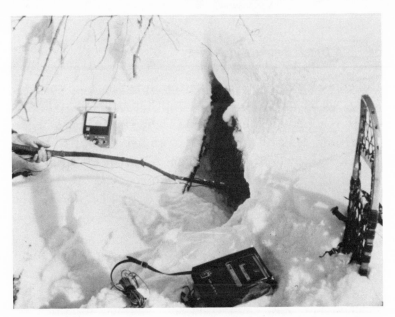

New York State researchers prepare to record sounds from a den.
(John O'Pezio)

already, only two of the orphaned cubs were selected
for the fostering project; the other was later sent to
another state. By this time it was early March and the
Catskill bears were due soon to emerge from hibernation. Before this happens, bears become less sleepy and
more aware of what is going on around them. Luckily
for the fostering project, a cold spell hit, which returned the awakening bears to the deep sleep of midwinter. Two of the cubs were collected and put in a
Styrofoam container (Styrofoam is a heat insulator) for
their trip to the northern Catskills. The five-week-old
animals each now weighed a little over 4 pounds (2
kilograms).

The Catskills were covered with snow that year.
After driving to the area of the den, the researchers
made the last part of the trip on snowshoes, carrying

the cub container. Everyone remained as quiet as possible, so as not to alert the mother bear. Just as the party reached the den, however, the young bears began squalling. Hastily, they were removed from the container and lowered into the den. A mirror positioned to reflect the inside of the den showed the researchers that the mother was undisturbed by the noise. She shifted slightly as she dozed to gather in the newcomers.

Six weeks later, in mid-April, a camera placed near the den's entrance showed the mother and cubs leaving. On several occasions after this, an airplane tracked her, and each time she was accompanied by three cubs. The New York researchers now think that in spite of all the noise that had initially come from the den, there probably was only one cub of the mother's, and that the others later seen with her were the foster cubs. The same group of researchers later placed two other orphaned cubs with another bear foster mother in the Catskills, and in that case, too, the mother accepted the cubs.

The best information we have on the development of young black bears comes from two cubs that were captured at an early age in 1970. In mid-April of that year, a pair of thin, weak, black-bear female cubs were found alone in Great Smoky Mountains National Park. Their mother had probably been killed by poachers. As the cubs had probably been born about the end of January, they were presumably two and a half months old. They weighed just 2 pounds (.9 kilograms) each, a low weight for bears this age, but despite their weakened condition they gave the park ranger who found them painful bites on the hands.

This frightened black bear cub was captured by North Carolina researchers during a forest fire. It weighed just seven pounds. (Joe Hamilton, North Carolina Wildlife Resources Commission)

Dr. Gordon M. Burghardt, a member of the Department of Psychology at the nearby University of Tennessee, heard about the cubs soon after they were found. He had become interested in black bears since coming to the area a few years before, but he found that books and scientific journals contained little information on the development of the animal. Observing two cubs would fill in many gaps in knowledge of the bear. Although Burghardt's primary interest is reptile behavior, he temporarily dropped his reptile work and took over the rearing of the two cubs. A number of Burghardt's graduate students helped in the project.

For the first few months of captivity, Kit and Kate, as the cubs were named, lived in the Burghardt home. At first they were fed warm cow's milk and honey every two hours; after a few days, the time between feedings was lengthened, until the cubs were eating

New York State researchers wear heavy gloves while feeding an abandoned cub. (Stephen Clarke, New York State Department of Environmental Conservation)

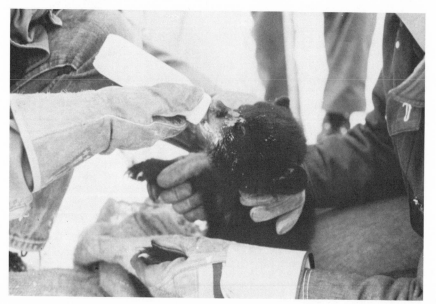

three meals a day. By the end of April, they were also taking solid baby food. Chewable items, such as apples and dog biscuits, were added a little later. The cubs showed no interest in meat until they were about four months old, when they began eating frankfurters and canned dog food.

By July, when they each weighed about 30 pounds (13.6 kilograms), the cubs were eating dry dog food, along with fruits and vegetables. They started gnawing on bones about this time, too. But it wasn't until several months later, when they were seven or eight months old, that they began to eat large amounts of meat and fish.

Very early the bears developed a curious way of eating their food, which was served to them in a dish on the floor. They turned the dish over, particularly if it had liquid in it, then lapped up the contents from the floor. Burghardt thinks this way of eating is similar to the way bears in the wild turn over logs and stones to look for insects; outside, in the yard, he noticed, the cubs turned over the same kinds of objects. Since they had never seen their mother do this, Burghardt thinks such behavior may not have to be learned in bears — it's instinctive.

Like the cubs observed in the wild, Kit and Kate began climbing early. By the end of April, when they were about three months old, they were climbing trees in the Burghardt backyard. From the first, they were very agile in trees and rarely slipped. Soon they stayed in the trees for hours, even when it was dark or raining. The arrival of a stranger invariably sent them to the base of a tree or up it if they were outside. Inside the house, the cubs climbed everywhere. One of their

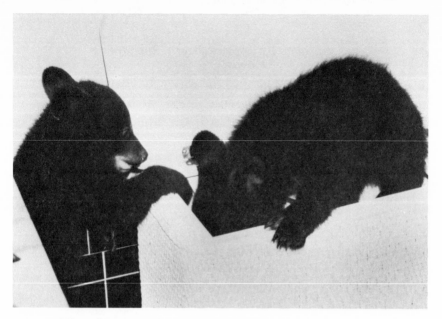

Kit and Kate at play. (Gordon Burghardt)

favorite tricks was to get up on a light wooden chair, which would topple over with a crash when they reached the top.

From the first day the cubs spent in the Burghardt house, they sought out dark places, such as the inside of kitchen cabinets, the clothes dryer, and the laundry hamper. They soon learned to manipulate the latches on the doors to these hideaways by hooking their front claws around any part of the door they could grasp. A stranger's approach inside the house often sent them to one of their hideaways, but they also went into them to play or relax.

Playing started early, too. Most of the young bears' games looked like play fighting. They would wrestle each other around, swatting with their front paws. There was one significant difference between play fighting and real fighting: when the bears were playing, they made no noise, but when they were fighting, they made several kinds of sounds. Sometimes the cubs played with Burghardt or other people, and when they did, they were much more gentle than when playing with each other. They seemed to realize people are more fragile than bears.

After several months with Burghardt, Kit and Kate moved to a roomy enclosure inside Great Smoky Mountains National Park. For the next few years Burghardt and a number of his graduate students carried out studies of the bears at the enclosure. The results of some of their work appear in this book.

About the time Burghardt and his students were observing various behaviors in Kit and Kate, Stephen Herrero and a colleague, J. D. Henry, were investigat-

Bear cub reared by Gordon Burghardt weighs in at ninety pounds. Ellis Bacon holds the cub. (Gordon Burghardt)

ing both captive- and wild-bear play in Canada. Some of their work was carried out at the Calgary Zoo. Their findings confirmed what Burghardt had discovered when Kit and Kate were still in his home: most of the play seen in the Canadian black bears was a kind of mock fighting, and the play involved no noise. The only noise the Canadian researchers heard the playing bears make was a low moan. If the other bear kept on playing after the moaning, the moaner usually attacked it.

The Canadian team took careful observations of the facial expressions young bears use in play fighting, and compared them with expressions used in real fighting. One of the differences they found was in the ears. Bears, like dogs and some other animals, can move their ears, and they use the position of the ears for communication among themselves. The researchers found five different ear positions, each of which seems to mean something to bears. During an aggressive encounter, for instance, the bears flattened their ears completely. In play, the ears might be partly flattened, but if one bear flattened them completely, the other bear stopped playing and might even run away.

Young bears follow a definite sequence in their play fighting, the Canadian observations show. First they try to knock the other bear off balance, usually by pawing at it. Sometimes both bears stand on their back legs to carry out these pawing matches. After one bear is knocked off balance, the other delivers a bite or quick swipe with its claws. The bears are careful not to hurt each other; in bites, the jaws are closed very gently around the opponent's neck or limb, and the clawing is done with the pad of the foot, not the claws.

According to Herrero, during bears' first two years

they may spend up to a few hours at a time in this kind of play. After that, they play less, although sub-adult bears (two to four years) are occasionally seen playing with other sub-adults of the same size.

All the studies made of black-bear behavior in the wild show that despite its early playing, this is a solitary animal; it spends most of its life alone. The only long-term relationship black bears have with other members of their species takes place in the family unit. Mothers and cubs spend the first year and a half of the cubs' life together. Although adult males and females spend a few days in each other's company during the mating period, after mating they pay no more attention to each other. Fathers have no role in bringing up their cubs. In fact, since males and females mate with a number of partners, it's usually hard to say which male is the father of a particular cub.

There are a few breaks in this solitary life aside from those just named. Adult bears may encounter one another on occasion when feeding in a dump or berry patch. When this happens, the feeding bears usually stay several hundred yards apart and do not bother one another. Sometimes, though, one bear may threaten the others. This happens most often when there is one large male bear and a number of smaller males and females. But females occasionally dominate males in a feeding situation. Stephen Herrero saw a female at a dump dominate all the males, even the largest.

All who have watched black-bear families agree that female bears are very solicitous of their cubs. Mother and young are seldom apart. The bear mother Herrero watched was never more than five feet from her cub, except when she was gathering nest material. If her cub cried while she was gone, she returned to its side within a minute. This surveillance continued even when the cub was able to run and climb trees. On several occasions, a person other than Herrero (whom the bears had become used to) came too close to the cub, and the mother made aggressive warning sounds and movements (see Chapter VII for a description of this behavior).

Charles Jonkel and Ian McT. Cowan, who studied the black bear in Montana, were threatened by a black-bear mother when they were tagging cubs. She finally became so aggressive that they had to tranquilize her.

Michigan state biologist El Harger had a similar experience when he and several other men were trying to release a cub that had been accidentally caught in a coyote trap. When the cub squalled, the mother rushed the group, making threatening sounds. The men yelled and waved their arms (both these actions are recommended for scaring off aggressive black bears) and the bear retreated. But as soon as the men tried again to free the cub, the mother rushed them again. She had to be restrained in another coyote trap.

In spite of this experience, Harger says that only a few females have tried to run him off when he was working with their cubs. More often, the bear mother would simply circle around in the brush, making threatening sounds. Nevertheless, Harger advises unarmed persons who come across a mother and her cubs to avoid them and leave the area without delay. Few mothers attack, he notes, but it is impossible to guess which ones will not and which will.

The threatening sounds and actions made by the

mother bears in the incidents just described all occurred when the cub was on the ground, where it is most vulnerable. If it can, a black-bear cub will run for a tree when danger threatens, while the mother either stands at the base of the tree to assess the danger or climbs the tree herself. Trees thus function as a kind of escape hatch for black bears. They also serve as a kind of baby sitter; when a mother bear wants to go off on her own for a short period, she encourages her cubs to stay in a tree during her absence. Stephen Herrero believes that the use of trees by black bears helps account for the high survival rate among cubs. Some researchers have found that ninety-five per cent of black-bear cubs survive during the period they are with their mother.

Black-bear mothers and cubs make a number of sounds to communicate with one another. Very small

If this cub feels threatened, it will immediately climb the tree. (National Park Service)

cubs make a kind of loud purring noise when they are nursing. I heard this noise at a Pennsylvania bear den and it reminded me of a well-tuned motor running. When they are uncomfortable or frightened, very young cubs make noises ranging from a thin, ghostly wail, like that of a breeze, to a loud crying, similar to that of human babies. In a Pennsylvania swamp, cubs crying in a den beneath a tree root were clearly audible to me about a hundred feet away. As they get older, cubs cry with even more volume.

Mother bears often call their cubs with a huffing noise, made by expelling the breath explosively from the mouth. This noise also accompanies other behavior, such as aggression.

For the first few weeks after mother and cubs have left the den, at the end of winter, the family stays close to the den site. Gradually, the family moves farther and farther away, though still remaining in the general area. The bear family observed by Herrero moved only about 200 feet from its den after leaving it for good.

In the fall, studies have shown, the bear mother is more active than all other bears. Sometimes she takes long trips away from home accompanied by her cubs. The reason for this increased activity isn't known, but it may have to do with the mother's role as teacher, protector, and provider.

Lynn Rogers, the Minnesota researcher, monitored a nursing bear mother with three cubs during 1975. The mother spent most of her active hours looking for food for herself and her cubs. Since nuts and berries were scarce in Minnesota that year, the mother depended on ants and hornets to supply the family with fat and protein. She moved from log to log, smelling some, turning others over, tearing still others apart. The three cubs were never seen by Rogers to open a log themselves, but they crowded eagerly around logs the mother opened and ate the food she revealed.

Although young cubs begin eating a variety of foods as soon as they emerge from the den, they continue to nurse until they are about seven months old. A few cubs nurse much longer. Yet even before they are weaned, young cubs are capable of surviving on their own. There are cases of five-and-a-half- to six-month-old cubs losing their mother and surviving. Cubs this age may weigh as little as 18 pounds (8 kilograms). Nevertheless, the rate of survival of orphaned cubs is not high.

Father bears play no active role in the life of their cubs, but their presence may help them indirectly. In some areas, males maintain territories (see Chapter V), fighting off other males that attempt to trespass. Since there are a few records of males' killing and eating cubs, this kind of cannibalism might be more frequent if males could wander everywhere. Wandering males would probably also compete with the female and her offspring for food.

Mothers and their cubs spend the second winter of the cubs' life together in the den. When the cubs enter the den at this time, they weigh 30 to 100 pounds (13.6 to 45 kilograms). When they re-emerge, as yearlings (animals over a year old), their weight ranges from about 40 pounds (18 kilograms) to over 100. Shortly thereafter, the male cubs may be as big as the adult females; many visitors to national parks mistake male

Three yearling cubs and their mother (third from left) at Crater Lake National Park. (National Park Service)

yearlings for adult females. In spite of the yearlings' size, however, their mother's care seems as solicitous as ever. The family is seldom separated.

Then, in the late spring or early summer of the cubs' second year, something happens to the black-bear family. The relatives that were inseparable for a year and a half suddenly part; each goes its own way. They may meet again by accident but they will never again form a family unit, except in rare cases. The young females usually stay within their mother's territory, or close to it, for the rest of their lives, but the young males eventually move away from it.

What breaks up the close-knit bear family at this time of year?

It is the mother bear's physiological condition. She is

about to go into her fertile period, estrus. Unless they are nursing — which prevents estrus — all adult black-bear females in North America enter this period in the summer, usually in June or July. Estrus lasts a short time, perhaps only four days. When the female goes into estrus, she gives off an odor that informs males of her condition. Males then seek her out and mate with her.

Researchers who have observed black bears aren't sure if the female drives her cubs out as she goes into estrus or if the male bear disperses them by his arrival. Evidence that Lynn Rogers collected in Minnesota indicates that it is the mother who engineers the event. Residents of a cabin near the home of a bear family reported to Rogers that they heard sounds like those bears use in fighting. Three hours after that, Rogers picked up radio signals showing that the three cubs in the family had departed. A few hours later, each of the three was a half mile away from the others. Neither the mother nor the young ever got together again, in spite of the fact that they saw one another often at a dump where they all fed — the same feeding dump to which, only a few days before the breakup, the mother had led all three of her cubs.

Rogers has tracked a number of mother bears from the time of the breakup through mating. Immediately after the breakup, he found, the female begins to cover much more ground in her territory than she did while her cubs were with her. Before any of these females had gone very far, they were joined by a male. Males also move much more than they had before the females went into estrus, and most of their travels take them through the territories of fertile females.

Males apparently follow scent trails laid down by the estrous females. From an airplane, Rogers watched several males following such trails. One male walked rapidly along the exact route that had been taken an hour before by a female in estrus. When he got close to her, she lifted her head, ran a short distance, stopped, then ran a little farther as the male kept approaching. The male continued and the female walked away, but very slowly. Within a minute, he had caught up to her and mated with her. The female continued to walk during the mating, eventually disappearing into a dense thicket.

Bears mate in the same way as dogs and many other four-footed animals. The male places his front legs on the female's back while he thrusts his penis into the female's vagina.

While the bears Rogers was watching were mating, another male bear, larger than the first, appeared and followed the couple into the brush. At this point, Rogers's airplane needed fuel, so he returned to his base. When he returned to the area, radio signals from the first male's collar showed he was more than 300 feet (91 meters) away from the female. Footprints from the larger male and the female led into the thicket and Rogers could hear the sounds of their mating.

After mating, females and males remain together for only a short period; the longest Rogers found was five days. Most couples part in a day or two. Both males and females mate with a number of partners, but since females are in estrus for only a few days, they have less chance than males of finding multiple partners. One male that Rogers tracked went into the territories of eight different females that had come into estrus. It isn't known if he mated with all of them, but some of them later had cubs.

Males often fight over females. Rogers has watched a number of these fights. In a few cases, large males simply chased away small males, but when the contestants were more evenly matched, the males battled for as long as four minutes, using both their claws and their teeth. The scenes of these battles were littered with clumps of fur and the vegetation was broken and trampled. Old males checked by the Minnesota researcher invariably had the scars of numerous battles on their shoulders, necks, and heads. Some also had injuries to the penis bone, a structure within the bear penis.

While the mother bear is mating, her offspring are suddenly on their own. The first few years after the family breakup are a difficult period for young bears. Not only is their mother not around to guide the yearlings, but the sons also usually seek an area far from the mother's territory, and their travels can lead to danger. In Lynn Rogers's study, half of the young males eventually moved more than 60 miles (96 kilometers) away from the mother. Traveling bears may cross heavily used roads, pass human dwellings, and almost certainly enter the territories of adult male black bears. In national parks, yearling males inevitably swell the ranks of panhandlers.

Studies show that more black bears, particularly males, die during this period than during any other. Mortality may run as high as fifty per cent.

Nevertheless, in most areas of the United States enough yearlings of both sexes survive to stabilize the black-bear population. The fortunes of one black-bear family that was tracked for eight years by Lynn Rogers show how this happens.

When Rogers's study started, in 1970, the mother bear, "A," was twenty years old, a very advanced age for a black bear. She had two cubs, a male and a female. A three-year-old female, A's daughter, shared a portion of her mother's territory. The mother separated from her cubs in the summer of 1971, but both stayed in part of their mother's territory.

In the fall, A's son and two daughters all made separate dens within the mother's territory. A had two more cubs that year, but killed them both in her den. Two days later she died of old age.

Three years after A's death, her seven-year-old daughter had her first litter. That fall there was little food, and A's other daughter, now four years old, did not breed, as her peak fall weight was low, about 145 pounds (66 kilograms); in Minnesota no female with a peak weight that low is known to have produced cubs that lived. A's grandchildren, however, survived and established territories of their own within their mother's. Again, there was so little food in the fall that neither of A's daughters had cubs that winter.

The following year, 1976, was the driest on record in northeastern Minnesota. Only one of A's children reproduced, her younger daughter, then seven years old. She had a single cub, which died soon after the mother came out of her den, in 1977.

In 1970, when Rogers first began to observe the bear family, there were three females and a male in A's territory. Eight years later, there was exactly the same number of each sex in the same territory.

CHAPTER V

The Black Bear at Home

At the top of a fire tower in Great Smoky Mountains
National Park, Howard Quigley, a graduate student at
the University of Tennessee, sweeps a mounted antenna around in a slow circle. There is a clicking noise,
sometimes soft, sometimes loud. When a signal becomes loud, Quigley keeps the antenna trained in its
direction and makes notations on a card. He wears
earphones to shut out other noises and hear the signals
more clearly.

"That's a really good signal," he says as the clicking
rises in volume. "It's Jackson, No. 409. Yesterday he
was on Skunk Ridge, over there, but today he's closer.
He's moved two miles in a day."

Using a control box, Quigley switches from Jackson's
frequency to that of another black bear. He is tracking
sixteen in all, each with a number, a name, and a radio
collar with its own frequency. He shows me a list with
such names as Apollo, Midnight, Godiva, Griz, Lauren,
Otis, and Jessie. All the bears were captured by Quigley and other graduate students of Dr. Michael Pelton's. After a radio collar was put on each animal, it
was released.

Four times a week, Quigley climbs the fire tower and

Howard Quigley tracks black bears from a fire tower in Great
Smoky Mountains National Park, and by means of a hand-held antenna and a portable receiver.

sweeps the antenna back and forth, picking up the
bears' radio signals. One day a month, the animals are
monitored for twenty-four hours.

Outside the tower, which is on a peak at the northern
end of the park, there is nothing to see but miles and
miles of green-covered mountains rolling off to the sky.
The Great Smoky Mountains, which are part of the
Appalachian Mountain Range, are composed of steep
hills, narrow valleys, and lush vegetation, straddling
the Tennessee–North Carolina border. The rainfall is
heavy and the temperatures are moderate. Much of the
terrain has thick underbrush, which, for people, makes
walking difficult. For bears, however, it is a good place,
and always has been, judging from the large numbers

that inhabited the area when the first white explorers arrived. The Smokies became a national park in 1934.

"We probably have four hundred and fifty to six hundred black bears in the park now, more than we used to think," says Quigley.

After an hour or so, he has picked up signals from all but two of his research subjects, including one he hadn't heard from in two weeks. Black bears in the Smokies, like black bears in most other areas, periodically roam outside their usual area in search of food. Griz, for instance, moved from near the fire tower to North Carolina, a distance of about 8 miles (13 kilometers), and stayed there for a month. Then he returned. Other radio-collared bears have made the same trip.

On top of the fire tower, Quigley can pick up signals for up to 18 miles (29 kilometers), because the tower is higher than the surrounding mountains. Standing on the ground, where the mountains rise all around, an observer with a hand-held antenna is limited to signals from at most 2 miles (3 kilometers) away. An airplane with antennae mounted on its wings does the best job of receiving signals; it can detect a bear 20 to 30 miles (32 to 48 kilometers) away.

In this project, Quigley has the part-time services of a plane flown by a park ranger off duty. The plane is flying on this particular day. When we climb down from the tower and walk back to Quigley's truck, we see it circling overhead. Quigley picks up a radio transmitter inside the truck and contacts the pilot. Both their voices are audible to me.

"Griz is over here between Parson's High Top and Hickory Top," says the pilot.

"That explains why I couldn't pick him up," says Quigley.

They exchange a few more remarks on the bears and then the plane flies off.

Quigley's study, he explains as we drive back through the park, is concerned with black-bear habitat, the physical surroundings of the bear. As one of the principal investigators in the project Quigley will track radio-collared animals for several years, noting their locations. From this information, he will calculate the animals' home ranges, the areas where they spend most of their time. Eventually, these data will be compared with vegetation maps by means of a computer, so that the bears' food, cover, and den utilization can be determined in detail.

Before radio telemetry was developed, studies of the movements of secretive wild animals, such as the black bear, were difficult to carry out, particularly in densely wooded areas like the Smokies. Quigley rarely sees his subjects, even when radio signals indicate they are very close to him. Few telemetry studies devoted solely to habitat have been completed as yet, but some earlier telemetry data include information on habitat. The information confirms, as had been suspected, that the black bear is a creature of forests or other dense areas of vegetation. But its preferences vary from area to area.

In the Smokies, a study has shown, bears choose oak and other hardwood forests, such as maple and beech. More than eighty per cent of all radio locations have been made in these areas. One reason for this preference is that berries, a favorite bear food, flourish in openings in hardwood forests in the summer. In the

A good bear habitat has dense underbrush for concealment. This thicket is in Great Smoky Mountains National Park. (University of Tennessee)

fall, hardwoods themselves furnish nuts and tree fruits such as cherries, both staples of the bear diet.

Pennsylvania black bears frequent both hardwood forests and softwood (pine, hemlock, spruce, tamarack) swamps. Bears along the southeastern coast of the United States also live in softwood swamps. In Florida, swamps favored by bears have dense clumps of a short tree called the titi, which forms a barrier almost impassable to people but not to bears; one of these bear swamps, in fact, has the name Impassable Swamp. Titi is often mixed with cypress in the Florida swamps.

In the northern United States, dense spruce-fir forests with many small natural and man-made clearings make up much of the black bear's habitat. The Southwest, compared with the rest of the country, is sparsely treed, but mountainous areas have thickets, called chaparrals, of evergreen shrubs and low trees, which bears inhabit. Chaparral can be almost as impassable as a titi swamp, and some Arizona chaparrals have more than one bear per square mile (2.6 square kilometers).

Although these habitats vary widely, they have several characteristics in common. They all contain dense underbrush for food and cover, and trees suitable for climbing. In fact, a map of North American forests is almost the same as a map of black-bear distribution. The only exception is Canada's Ungava Peninsula, where some black bears have recently moved into treeless areas; this is perhaps owing to the disappearance there of the grizzly bear, which sometimes preys on the black bear.

With that exception, the black bear stays close to trees. Canadian researcher Stephen Herrero points out that black bears are very reluctant to venture far from the shelter of trees, even for favorite foods. In black-bear country, garbage dumps located far from trees get few bear visitors, dumps near trees are comparatively crowded. Herrero once watched bears crossing an open area with several scattered large trees: the bears zigzagged across the space in order to pass by each tree.

The black bear needs trees but it does much of its feeding *below* trees, in the understory vegetation. This vegetation also furnishes the bear with the ground cover it needs. So a black bear prefers, not a mature forest composed of tall trees, whose shade prevents underbrush, but a younger, more open forest, where light enters and allows vegetation to grow beneath the trees and in clearings. A forest with small clearings, a forest with neighboring pastureland, and abandoned farmland returning to woods each offer the black bear the variety of food and cover it needs.

The kind of habitat a bear chooses is clearly shown in a recent telemetry study carried out in southeastern North Carolina by researchers from the University of Georgia and the North Carolina Wildlife Resources Commission. Almost half the study area is made up of "Carolina bays," small sunken sites that contain fruit and other bear food, but few trees. Bears were found to spend more time feeding in these bays than in any other location. About fourteen per cent of the area consists of swamps with a tangle of trees and shrubs, and this is where the bears spent much of their time in the

A 325-pound male North Carolina bear retreats through pine-oak woods after being tagged and measured. Woods grow on sand ridges connecting bays and swamps along the North Carolina coast. (Joe Hamilton, North Carolina Wildlife Resources Commission)

Montana bears feeding in an area cleared by loggers. (Montana Department of Fish and Game)

fall, when nuts are plentiful, though not during other seasons. If a bear is chased by hunters' dogs, however, it invariably retreats to the swamps, if possible. In these wet, densely vegetated areas, men and dogs have a hard time pursuing bears, and the bears have an excellent chance of survival.

What do bears eat?

Almost anything. One of the few foods bears aren't tempted by — it's untouched in snares — is liver. A New York State research team once caught a bear with bagels. Bears are omnivores, the term for animals that eat a wide variety of animal and vegetable foods. We are omnivores ourselves. "Omnivore" is a little misleading when applied to the black bear, however, because black bears mostly eat vegetable matter. A study in Maine based on the examination of bear scats shows that only one per cent of bear food is meat other than insects. In spring and fall, about half the bear's diet is vegetation, a proportion that rises to eighty per cent in the summer. Much of the noninsect animal matter that Maine bears eat is carrion — the bodies of animals that have died of starvation or other causes.

Maine bears also eat a lot of garbage when they get the chance. In the summer, when there are many tourists in the state, about fifteen per cent of the average Maine bear's diet is composed of garbage. Although these figures come from just one state, they are typical of statistics on the bear diet gathered elsewhere. A study by Larry Beeman and Michael Pelton in Great Smoky Mountains National Park and nearby areas shows that grasses, herbs, berries, and nuts make up eighty-one per cent of the bear's food; animal matter, most of it bees and beetles, is eleven per cent; and garbage and other artificial foods are eight per cent. The panhandling of a few bears probably accounts for most of the statistics on artificial foods eaten by these bears.

The foods black bears eat vary with the seasons. When they first come out of their dens, in the spring, bears depend mostly on grasses and weeds, along with the carrion of animals that have died during the winter. Throughout the summer in most parts of the United States, bears dine on blackberries, blueberries, huckleberries, and insects. Some of these berries are still eaten in early fall, along with late-ripening species such as the gallberry, a bear favorite in the Southeast.

Bears also eat fruits in early fall, such as black cherries. Late fall brings a rich diet of nuts for the bears to fatten on as the denning season draws near.

Certain foods are particularly popular with bears in certain areas because of their availability. In Washington State, skunk cabbage is plentiful in the spring and this plant turns up in the scats and stomachs of many bears. Squawroot, a parasite on tree roots, is a common spring plant in the Smokies, where bears consume it in large amounts. In Vermont, many white-tailed deer die over the winter, and bears eat their carcasses in the spring. Since spring is a period when fewer foods are available and bears are hungry because of their long hibernation, it is the season when they are most likely to prey on other wild animals and even domestic livestock. In Montana a bear may on occasion eat a lamb, sheep, or calf in spring.

Bears may also prey on livestock in the summer but another type of predation is much more common — raiding commercial beehives for honey. In states such as Georgia, bears can be a big problem for some beekeepers. Some other specialized summer foods are the grape-sized purple fruit of the salal bush in Washington State, the berries of the evergreen shrub manzanita in California, and the fruit of the mountain-ash tree in Idaho. Summer is also the time when bears in national parks and other vacation areas consume the greatest quantity of artificial food, which they beg or steal.

One of the bear's favorite fall foods in North Carolina is the fruit of the black-gum tree. The long-lasting mountain-ash fruit plays the same role in fall in Idaho. Some bears turn to apple orchards and corn fields during this season; in Vermont, apples are one of the most important foods for bears in September, October, and November, and some years bears are still pawing apples out of the snow in December. Alaskan black bears catch salmon during the fish's spawning season, autumn, although they don't eat as much of this fish as does their relative, the grizzly. In Maine in fall, bears eat a fish called the white sucker.

Bears eat more and gain weight faster during late summer and fall than at any other time of the year. In the Montana study conducted by Charles Jonkel and Ian Cowan, bears in fall gained an average of .84 pound (.4 kilogram) per day over a thirty-day period. One female gained 1.55 pounds (.7 kilogram) per day. Bears are capable of even greater weight gains than these. In the Catskills, for instance, a male bear put on nearly 4 pounds (2 kilograms) a day over twenty-four days — a total of 92 pounds (42 kilograms). The reason bears gain so much weight during the late summer and fall is to prepare for the long fast of winter in the den. Without ample fat reserves, bears might not make it through hibernation.

The ways bears eat have been studied by Ellis Bacon and Gordon Burghardt of the University of Tennessee, who observed the captive black bears Kit and Kate consuming some of the basic foods of their species. When one of these bears was picking an acorn from a tree, she would extend her tongue and grasp the nut between her tongue and upper lip, which would be pushed forward for the purpose. With berries, the bear would grasp the fruit just behind her front teeth and then pull back her head to break the berry off the stem. Sometimes the tongue was used to guide the berry into the mouth; paws were used only to hold the bush or tree. The front paws were used much more in eating grass, not only to hold it down while the bear ate, but also to rake through it and lift it closer to the mouth.

To obtain insects and other foods buried in the ground, the bear would dig with one paw at a time, pulling the earth toward her body, never away from it. The same motion was used to overturn logs and rocks: the bear would grasp the side of the object farthest away and pull it upward and back toward her body. With small moving prey, such as insects and mice, the bear would generally slap at it with a paw a number of times, crushing it. Sometimes the bear used both paws to grab the prey on the ground and crush it.

Bacon and Burghardt conclude, rather admiringly, that the black bear is a neat and even delicate eater. It seldom consumes debris, spitting out items like cores and stems, or avoiding them altogether.

Black bears can create somewhat of a mess in certain feeding situations, however. Larry Beeman and Michael Pelton watched black bears feeding in fruit and nut trees. Both adults and young climbed the trees and then either pulled the limbs in with their paws or else broke or chewed the limbs off and dropped them to the ground. Some of the tossed limbs were as thick as 4 inches (10 centimeters). By attacking the limbs in this way, the bears could get at otherwise unreachable fruits and nuts. Although Beeman and Pelton conclude that bears do some harm to trees, the scientists believe the damage is slight compared with that of storms.

Black-bear feeding activity is so characteristic of the animal that evidence of it is one of the surest signs that bears are in an area. In a Georgia study by Robert Ernst, of the Georgia Department of Natural Resources, the most common bear signs found were dug-up yellow-jacket and ant nests and turned-over logs and rocks; the ground beneath the rocks and logs had been scratched by claws, although not actually excavated. Other familiar bear signs are twisted and broken branches of such trees as cherry, apple, beech, and oak, along with claw marks on the trees' trunks.

Food and cover, as well as denning sites (which are treated in Chapter VI), are a black bear's main requirements in choosing its range, the area where it spends most of its time. A bear usually maintains its range for many years, and when removed from it makes a strong effort to return "home." Before radio telemetry had been developed, studies of black-bear movements involved capturing, tagging, and releasing the animals (see Chapter I), many of which were problem bears that were moved to a different area before release. Such studies, which are still being carried out, furnish valuable information on homing.

In a recapture study conducted in Michigan some years ago, a female black bear homed 142 miles (229 kilometers) from her release site to where she had been captured. This is the longest distance ever homed by a black bear. But a young male in Idaho came close, homing 140 miles (225 kilometers) in a 1977 study. The most determined homers of all may have been three bears put on an island a half mile out in Bonavista Bay, Newfoundland: the bears swam through rough waters to shore and then walked 11 miles (17.7 kilometers) to get home. Homing movements of more than 100 miles are very unusual, but both recapture and telemetry studies show that many bears return 20 or 30 miles (32 or 48 kilometers) to their home. A committee of black-bear experts recently suggested that problem bears be moved a minimum of 75 miles (121 kilometers) to be sure they did not home.

Most homing bears move just a few miles homeward each day, but some go much faster. A California bear was transported 70 miles (112 kilometers) from a campground where it had been causing problems; on the eighth day after the move, California state biologist Tim Burton saw the bear peeking around a tree in the same campground where it had been caught. A Virginia female bear named Rambling Rose took just eleven days to walk the 130 miles (209 kilometers) from where she had been released to where she had been captured. Earlier, Rambling Rose made a 60-mile (97-kilometer) trip in four days.

The ability of black bears to home has been known for many years, but bear researchers still don't know exactly how they manage the feat. Some important new information on the subject comes from the studies of radio-collared bears carried out in the mid-1970s by Gary Alt, who is now with the Pennsylvania Game Commission. Two of the homing bears Alt tracked were an adult female and her cub, captured as nuisance bears and airlifted 14 miles (23 kilometers) away. Another of the female's cubs was left in the female's home range. Recapture studies have indicated that being separated from their cubs motivates mother bears to home, and the movements of this Pennsylvania female support this finding.

As Alt radio-tracked the bears from the air, he occasionally caught sight of them. Each time, they were less than 80 feet (25 meters) apart and the mother was always in the lead. Her movements took the pair in a

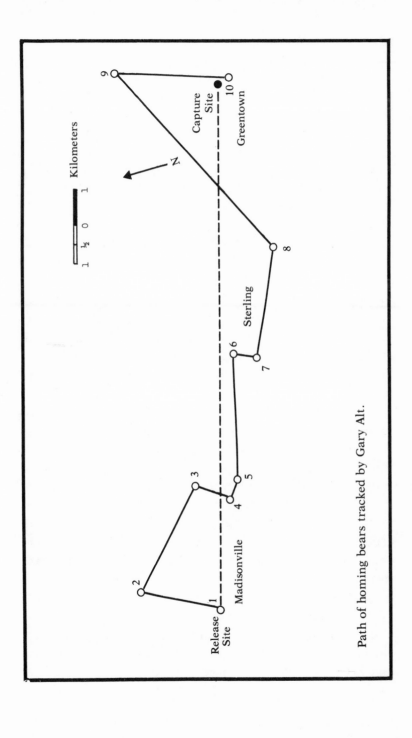

Path of homing bears tracked by Gary Alt.

zigzag path: first she went in a direction perpendicular to a homeward track, then she went directly toward home. This happened several times. Within seventy-seven hours, the two were back at the capture site, reunited with the other cub.

Alt gathered some even more intriguing homing data when he followed a radio-collared adult male on foot. Like the female, this bear was a nuisance animal, which had been captured and then released in another area. The distance he homed was 19 miles (31.6 kilometers). At first, Alt observed, the bear wandered in a direction almost perpendicular to a homeward path. After going less than a mile, however, the bear stopped and began sidestepping with his front feet, pivoting around his hind feet. He had almost completed two full circles when he stopped with his body turned in a homeward direction. Then he began walking in that direction.

After traveling only a few hundred yards, the bear repeated the circling pattern, and again left the circle in a homeward direction. In less than a mile, the same thing happened once more.

Alt made the rest of his observations of the bear from the air. The animal didn't continue in a homeward direction after the circling behavior but wandered around the release site for three days. Then he suddenly began moving out on the track he had started three days earlier. Less than a week after his capture, he was home.

Alt believes the circling behavior he observed in the male bear had something to do with his ability to home: homing bears, he suggests, may get their bearings this way. As yet, there isn't enough evidence to prove or disprove the theory. Other bear researchers believe that black bears may home by making random movements in unfamiliar terrain; eventually, these movements take them into familiar terrain. Bears do often take long trips outside their range, and these travels may familiarize them with different areas.

Telemetry studies provide information not only on bear homing but also on the size of bear ranges, the way the ranges change over time, and how much the ranges overlap. Although the 142-mile homing record was set by a female, telemetry data show males normally move farther than females and have larger ranges. The largest range found for a bear was a 227-square-mile (588 square kilometers) area occupied by an adult New York male. An adult Michigan male had a home range of 107 square miles (266.5 square kilometers). Dental problems were noted when the Michigan bear was radio-collared, and the discomfort of this condition may have been responsible for its unusually long movements.

Some other large home ranges that have been found are 60 square miles (155 square kilometers) in North Carolina, 78 square miles (202 square kilometers) in Pennsylvania, and 85 square miles (221 square kilometers) in West Virginia. All were of adult males.

Most bear ranges, however, are smaller than these. Richard J. Poelker and Harry D. Hartwell, of the Washington State Game Department — who conducted one of the first radio-telemetry studies of black bears — found that males in Washington had an average range of 19.9 square miles (51.7 square kilometers); females had an average range of 2.04 square miles (5.2 square kilometers). In Idaho, Steven Amstrup, of the Univer-

Idaho male bears, like this four-year-old tagged by John Beecham, have a mean range of 45 square miles. (John Beecham, Idaho Department of Fish and Game)

sity of Idaho, and John Beecham, of the Idaho Department of Fish and Game, estimated that males had a mean range of 45 square miles (112 square kilometers) and females 21 square miles (49 square kilometers). Some of the smallest male ranges in the United States are in Great Smoky Mountains National Park, where average ranges for males are just 4.2 square miles (11 square kilometers) and for females, 2.6 square miles (6.7 square kilometers).

The quality of the habitat probably explains most, if not all, of the difference in range size for bears of the same sex, researchers believe. In areas where ranges are small, the food supply is plentiful, varied, and concentrated. In areas where ranges are large, there is less food, it is less varied, and it is scattered throughout the range: to find enough to eat in a poor habitat, a bear must cover more ground.

The difference in range size between males and females probably arises from the difference in the strategy the two sexes adopt in mating, some researchers speculate. A male mates with many females, so it is an advantage for him to have a large range that includes the ranges of many females. A female, on the other hand, mates with only a few males, so it is to her advantage to have a range that is just big enough for herself and her young. One piece of evidence that supports this theory is that when females have young, they occupy a bigger range than they do when they are by themselves.

Apart from such expansion and contraction, female-bear ranges, once established, tend to stay much the same. This may not be true of male ranges. A telemetry study carried out in Idaho (by Doyle G. Reynolds, now with the Idaho Department of Fish and Game, and John Beecham) found that over a two-year period, adult-male ranges shifted considerably. In 1976, one adult male moved his range almost completely out of his 1975 range — the two ranges overlapped only slightly.

A phenomenon that complicates the range picture is seasonal movements. In areas such as Great Smoky Mountains National Park, some bears have two different ranges: a year-round, or home, range, where they spend most of the year, and a seasonal range, which they cover mostly in the fall. Every fall, some bears move long distances to their seasonal range, and then late in the fall they return to their home range, to den. When Michael Pelton's students compared the vegetation of the home ranges with that of the seasonal ranges, they found many more nut-producing trees, such as oaks, in the fall ranges, which affords some explanation for the seasonal travel.

The same "fall shuffle," as Pelton calls it, occurs in Minnesota. Lynn Rogers found one old male bear that moved 125 miles (201 kilometers) in search of acorns during the fall, then returned to his home range to den. A Minnesota female with cubs moved 57 miles (92 kilometers) to a source of fall food.

Along with these regular seasonal movements, Great Smoky Mountains National Park is the scene of mass migrations of bears every few years, when some of the nut-producing trees fail. When this happened in 1972, at least forty bears were killed or trapped wandering in the three counties just outside the park; normally, only a few bears are killed in these areas. That same year, there was a big jump in the number of bear incidents in the park, too: bears approached campers to beg for food, panhandled on highways, stole food from backpacks, and generally made a nuisance of themselves. The next year, when nut crops were normal, the number of bear incidents went down again.

The sharing of ranges by bears has been established, but the extent to which it occurs still isn't clear. Telemetry and other studies have determined that in most cases, as mentioned, adult male bears have ranges that include those of a number of adult females. But there are different findings on adults' sharing ranges with members of the same sex. In Idaho and Tennessee, males have been found in the ranges of male bears, and females in the ranges of female bears.

By contrast, in Montana bears of the same sex generally avoid one another's ranges.

One reason bears of the same sex will share ranges probably has to do with the size of habitat available. In some areas of Great Smoky Mountains National Park, for instance, there simply isn't enough room for each bear to have a range to itself. The richness of the habitat may play a part in range sharing, too. Frederick G. Lindzey, of Utah State University, studied black bears on an island in Washington State where there is a large amount of food available in a small area; female-bear ranges on the island were small and overlapped.

Another possible reason for bears' sharing ranges has to do with their family relationships. Lynn Rogers found that the daughters of female bears in Minnesota usually took up permanent residence in part of their mother's range. Later, when the daughters became mothers, they were more likely to expand their range into a neighboring range. The sons of female bears often spent a year or two after the family breakup in their mother's range, but invariably they moved on by the time they were three and a half.

Adult female bears in the same range may, therefore, be related to one another. Because the daughters will be permanently sharing their mother's range, the mother usually expands her range when she becomes pregnant for the first time. She expands it even more during her second pregnancy.

Rogers discovered that female bears defend their range against unrelated females and possibly also against males outside the breeding season. When an animal occupies a range by itself and defends it, the range is called a territory. On several occasions, Rogers saw females in a territory chasing intruding females out of it, although he never saw an actual fight. On other occasions, though, intruding females simply retreated when they saw the female that occupied the territory. Rogers also witnessed a very large male hurrying away from a small female within her territory.

The way in which bears recognize one another's presence in an area isn't clear, but it probably has to do with scent. The scent is often found on a "bear tree," one of the most common signs of the black bear. This is a tree that has been clawed, rubbed, and bitten repeatedly by bears, often over a period of years; some of the bark is torn off and there are usually bear hairs stuck in the tree's resin. Bear trees are almost always located near trails or other places where bears travel. A bear tree Howard Quigley pointed out to me in Great Smoky Mountains National Park was just off a logging road that bears often used at night.

Lynn Rogers has observed radio-collared black bears marking trees in Minnesota. Most of them were males, and they marked much more often in the breeding season than at any other time. One eleven-year-old male marked a tree by standing on his hind legs and rubbing his back on the trunk; at intervals, he twisted his head around to bite the trunk. When the bear found a signpost lying on the ground, he squirmed around on it on his back with all four feet in the air and bit the sign a few times. Every such tree or sign that Rogers found was either at the junction of a logging road or at the place where the road entered a swamp frequented by bears.

Rogers examined the trees right after the bears had marked them, and found that the scent of bear was strong enough for him to smell. Since bears have a much better sense of smell than people do, Rogers believes bear trees can be smelled by the animals for a long time after they have been marked. The trees in the study were usually marked during the mating season, when male bears are most aggressive, which leads Rogers to think that the trees may warn males that other males are in the area, so that they can avoid a fight. The fact that the bear trees Rogers found were all in the territories of estrous females or near garbage dumps — both bear attractants — seems to support his theory.

How females recognize the territories or ranges of other females isn't known, since they seldom mark trees, but females probably deposit some scent on foliage as they move, Rogers believes. These scents, however, don't last as long as the male ones on bear trees.

Along with yielding information on bear ranges, telemetry studies have revealed the times of activity in the bear's daily life. It used to be believed that all black bears were nocturnal, or night-active, but it is now seen that in some areas, bears are more active by day, in other areas by night. Bears can also change this pattern of activity. David Garshelis, a student of Michael Pelton's, broke down the activity of bears in Great Smoky Mountains National Park by season. In spring, bears were most likely to be active around sunrise and sunset; they were completely inactive at night. With the coming of summer, bears became active at midday, too, but they remained inactive at night. In the fall, bears were as active by day as by night.

Garshelis believes that these seasonal differences

may be due to the food supply. In the spring, he points out, bears are at their lowest weight, and the only foods available are low-nutrition grasses and herbs; to save energy, the bears eat for only part of the day and rest the remainder of the time. In the summer, there is plenty of food, so bears can afford to spend most of the day eating, mating, and patrolling their ranges. By fall, bears must put on the bulk of their weight, so they spend most of their time eating, night and day. The winter days and nights are spent in hibernation.

Studies in the Smokies and other areas also make clear that no matter when bears are active, most bears will take pains to avoid people. In West Virginia where bears are most active during the day, it has been found that they cross roads mainly at night. In Great Smoky Mountains National Park, where there are many hikers and cars, bears make more use of trails and roads in the nighttime, even though they are generally active during the day. It is because bears usually keep out of sight during the day that the animal seems completely nocturnal. Now, thanks to telemetry, we know otherwise.

CHAPTER VI

The Black Bear's
Long Winter Sleep

Bear biologist Gary Alt, of the Pennsylvania Game
Commission, stops his van in front of a handsome
house on a large, wooded lot. It is part of a vacation-
house development in Pennsylvania's Pocono Mountains, a popular resort area. I stop my car behind the
van and get out to join a group that includes Alt's father, Floyd, who has a contract with the state to track
the black bears his son is studying. The development
we are in seems to be an unlikely spot for a hibernating
black bear, but that's what the Alts say we will find
here.

"I'll just check with the home owner," says Gary Alt,
walking up the path to the house.

He returns in a few minutes and leads us into the
side yard. There is a large rock formation there. On the
side facing away from the road is a cleft in the rock,
next to a tree.

"Hear that sound?" says Gary Alt. "Cubs nursing."

It is a curious rumbling sound, like a small, well-
tuned motor running. Alt gets on his knees to look inside the cleft, holding a flashlight so that the interior
is illuminated. He beckons to us, and one by one we
creep up behind him and peer into the cleft. In the
darkness of the den, I see a black bear's pale snout

Yoko and her cubs spent the winter in this den near a house in the Pocono Mountains. Entrance is the narrow cleft between rock and tree at right.

moving back and forth. Her eyes are open and she looks directly at me. Below her head are what look like two pairs of shining dark eyes.

"Could the cubs' eyes be open?" I ask.

"This late in February they probably are," says Floyd Alt.

As we leave, the home owner is standing on his porch, watching the bear den with a proprietary air. He must be one of the few people in the United States with an occupied bear den just outside his door. Before we leave the development, the Alts show us the den that was used by the same bear, whom they have named Yoko, the year before. It is in a similar rock formation about ten feet from one of the roads running through the development. Yoko, who is about five

Gary Alt in the entrance of Yoko's former den, just a few feet from a road.

years old, was born in the development herself. Her mother probably chose the area as her range before it became a development.

Yoko was the culmination of a surprising day. Starting about nine o'clock that morning, the Alts had led our group to five different black-bear dens, each with a mother and several young cubs, born in January and February.

Pennsylvania has some 2000 to 3500 black bears, in several areas, one of them the mountainous northeastern region where the Alts operate. Gary Alt is involved in a long-term telemetry study of the animals that began when he was at Pennsylvania State University. When I visited him, in 1980, he was tracking twenty different bears; by summer, he expected the number to be fifty. That February, he was checking out his radio-collared females for new cubs. A few weeks later, when the cubs were old enough to take the disturbance, he put new collars on the mothers, with fresh batteries.

The first bear we visited that day in February was Sarah, who was sleeping under a pile of brush in a small clearing created by loggers. The brush gave her only partial protection from the weather, and she could clearly be seen. The head of one of her cubs was visible next to her body. There was a low grunting sound from the cubs when we first arrived, but the mother did not move or make a sound.

"She knows we're here, though," said Gary Alt as we stood looking at the pile of black fur beneath the brush heap.

The next bear had no name or radio collar. Gary Alt found her by checking a rock den that is usually occupied by a hibernating bear. The den was a low, rocky

Under this pile of brush in a Pennsylvania woods is a mother bear with her cubs.

cave near the top of a steep hill that was covered with snow. Alt lay down so he could see inside the opening and shone his flashlight around the interior.

"I can't see a thing but I hear one — she's got cubs," he announced.

We listened intently and then I heard it — a thin, ghostly cry, like a sigh or a breeze.

"The mother's moving around," said Alt after listening some more. "But she's not woofing [making a blowing sound], so she isn't aggressive."

Normally, he explained, as we went down the hill, adult black bears are alerted when someone looks into their den. They look up, move their head, occasionally make a warning sound. To change the mothers' collars he will give them a tranquilizing drug similar to the one used by the Catskill research team. Cubs born that year are too young to collar, but yearlings spending their second winter in a den sometimes get a collar, too. Floyd Alt makes all the collars used by the Alt team, with components from the Western Electric Company. The collars function for about a year.

The third bear we visited was Sharon. She had excavated her den on a steep hillside, possibly expanding the den of a smaller animal. The opening was small, so small I wondered how a full-grown female bear could squeeze herself inside. Gary Alt crouched at the opening with the flashlight. I looked in over his shoulder and saw nothing but a leaf-strewn floor, because the bear was at the back of the den. I heard something, though — loud cries like those of a human baby. They were much louder than the ones we had heard at the previous den, indicating that the cubs were somewhat older.

The fourth bear on our list, Heidi, was in a blueberry swamp behind one of the old farmhouses that are still very numerous in northeastern Pennsylvania. The exact location of the den was in doubt. A month earlier, Gary Alt explained, he had frightened Heidi out of her old den, so he wasn't sure where she was now. Floyd Alt had brought along a hand-held antenna and he held it aloft as we moved into the swamp. The antenna gave off a high, whistling series of beeps. When the beeps got louder, Gary Alt took the instrument and went off on his own, so that the group wouldn't alarm the bear.

He was back shortly. "She's right at the base of that old snag over there," he said, indicating a dead tree a few hundred feet from us. "It's the same den she was in before and she's got cubs. They're squalling."

From the direction of the snag came a bawling noise, like that of a dozen very angry human babies. It was amazingly loud.

"We'd better get out of here," said Gary Alt. "Heidi's a very nervous bear and I don't want her to abandon those cubs."

Our total for the day was five hibernating bears in six hours, plus cubs.

Until radio telemetry became available to researchers, finding this many bears in their dens in a single day would have been impossible. An occasional hunter, hiker, or biologist could track a hibernating bear — usually by following the animal's footprints in the snow — but most hibernators evaded notice. Today, researchers all over the country are tracking radio-collared bears to their dens and collecting information on the animals and the dens themselves. A few capture bears and study the hibernation process at close hand, both with and without telemetry. As a result of this work, a new picture of black-bear hibernation is emerging.

Some of the most basic findings in the physiology of black-bear hibernation come from an unusual application of radio telemetry developed at the University of Iowa. Iowa has few, if any, black bears, but Dr. G. Edgar Folk, Jr., of the Department of Physiology, and his colleagues have designed a tiny radio transmitter that can be placed within the body of large animals. It can measure both temperature and heartbeat. The whole unit, called the Iowa radio capsule, weighs from half an ounce to an ounce and a half (14 to 42.5 grams).

To place the unit inside a black bear, the animal is anesthetized and an incision is made in its abdomen.

The capsule is inserted and then anchored with surgical thread. After the operation, the bear feels no discomfort.

Because of the small number of batteries the radio capsule can carry, its power is limited, and a researcher must choose between studying the animal at very close range — using little energy — over a long period and studying the animal from farther away for a short period. Folk wanted to monitor the black bear's heart rate and temperature throughout the entire hibernation — which lasts a number of months — so he elected to study it at close range.

The Iowa radio capsule is only a little bigger than a quarter. It is implanted in the body of a bear to measure temperature and heartbeat. (G. Edgar Folk, Jr.)

Folk has carried out his bear-hibernation research at the Arctic Research Laboratory, in Barrow, Alaska, and at the Arctic Aeromedical Laboratory, in Fairbanks. For several winters, he put black bears carrying the implanted transmitters in unheated cages, one indoors and one outdoors. To encourage the animals to hibernate, he stopped giving them food, darkened their cages, and provided straw for bedding.

Under these conditions, the bears gradually began to change their physiological state. The normal sleeping heart rate of a black bear is about forty beats per minute. Soon after hibernation began, the rate, as shown by the Iowa radio capsule, decreased to thirty-two beats per minute. Then it went down to twenty beats per minute. Then to ten beats per minute. At this point in the animal's hibernation, the heart rate occasionally went down to eight beats per minute, the lowest registered. The whole process of changeover to the hibernating heart rate took two to four weeks, the radio capsule showed.

In most cases, a separate capsule was used to monitor body temperature. It did not show a dramatic change, like that of the heart-rate capsule. The normal temperature of black bears is about 100 degrees Fahrenheit (38 degrees centigrade). In hibernation, this temperature gradually dropped, but only to about 91 degrees Fahrenheit (34 degrees centigrade).

Folk was able to watch one of his hibernating subjects in its darkened cage through a special lens. He saw that the animal remained in a curled-up position, with the top of its skull resting against the bedding and the nose near the tail. If disturbed, it would lift its head, then go back to the same position.

None of Folk's bears ate any food or drank any liquid during the experimental hibernation, which lasted about three months (the animals were wakened before the natural end of hibernation in Alaska, where the period lasts seven months). After the bears left their dens, Folk examined the enclosures and found they had deposited no urine or feces.

An unusual phenomenon associated with the absence of eating, drinking, and elimination in hibernating black bears is what researchers call the fecal plug. This is a wad of material that is held within the bear's colon, or lower digestive track, throughout the period of hibernation. When the animal comes out of hibernation in the den, it deposits the fecal plug on the ground. Sometimes, too, the bear does this when it is disturbed from its sleep before the normal end of hibernation. A number of fecal plugs have been collected by scientists, and analyses of them show they are made up mostly of vegetation the bear ate just before hibernating, and hair. The hair apparently gets into the animal's body during the licking the bear does when it is in the den.

Folk's work helps clarify the differences between the hibernation of bears and that of the so-called true hibernators, all of which are small animals (the groundhog is the best known of this group). The true hibernators undergo an extreme drop in both temperature and heart rate, as well as a reduction in metabolism. But these animals wake up every four to ten days to urinate and defecate. Bears also undergo the extreme drop in heart rate and a reduction in metabolism, but their temperature does not drop dramatically and they do not urinate or defecate at all during hibernation. Another difference between the two groups is that bears go into hibernation slowly, but can be aroused quickly — Folk found that when a hibernating bear was wakened, its heart rate returned to normal in half an hour. True hibernators, by contrast, enter hibernation quickly and are slow to arouse.

In Folk's opinion, the bear is a deeper hibernator than the true hibernators, since the bear does not wake up periodically. "I believe that the hibernation observed in bears is an example which in the evolutionary sense is more perfected than that of small mammals," he says.

Another scientist who has carried out research on the physiology of black-bear hibernation is Dr. Ralph A. Nelson, a professor of nutrition at the University of Illinois. A physician, Nelson is interested in animal research that may benefit human health. He has analyzed the blood and urine of hibernating black bears and discovered that the reason the animal is able to go long periods without eating or drinking is that it uses its fat to produce both the calories and the water it needs. The bear avoids excreting waste by slowing down its metabolism of protein, the major source of the body's waste products. The small amount of urine that is produced is absorbed by the bladder.

At the end of hibernation, the black bear has lost between fifteen and twenty-five per cent of its weight — but all in fat, not lean tissue. Its lean body weight is just about the same as it was before hibernation.

One of the most remarkable feats the black bear accomplishes during this period, Nelson points out, is nursing its young when it is neither eating nor drinking. For this task, too, the bear mother apparently draws on her fat reserves. Bear milk has a very high fat content; it is between twenty-five and thirty-three per cent fat, compared with the three per cent fat of both human milk and cow's milk. Bear milk is also high in protein compared with human and cow's milk, and it is low in lactose, a substance in cow's milk to which many children are allergic.

Nelson used his findings to devise a special diet for human patients with defective kidneys. Normally, such patients must undergo a lengthy process called hemodialysis every few days to remove the waste products that their kidneys are unable to handle. When these patients were on the Nelson diet, their bodies created fewer waste products, so that the period between dialysis could be extended to about ten days. Nelson thinks the same kind of diet may also be helpful to space travelers, who have a problem disposing of the body's waste products in the tight confines of the spaceship.

Besides information on the processes of hibernation, new research is also telling us how black bears choose dens, what they do in them, and how long they stay in them.

Studies in various parts of the United States suggest that the period of time a black bear stays in its den depends largely on climate. In Alaska, black bears spend up to seven months in hibernation, from early October to sometime in May. Minnesota bears go into hibernation as early as September, but they are usually out by the beginning of April. Upper-Michigan bears begin denning about mid-October, lower-Michigan bears in late October. Idaho bears enter their dens in mid-October and come out in mid-April.

Northern-Montana bears are in their dens by late October but they do not come out until mid-May.

In warmer areas, black bears spend shorter periods in the den. A study of one bear in western Washington, which has a relatively mild climate, shows it went into hibernation in early November and was completely active again by early April. A female Pennsylvania bear did not go into her den until just after Christmas, and she was out again, with three cubs, on March 22. The earliest any bear denned in a North Carolina study was December 5, and the latest any bear came out was April 22. California, Arizona, and Tennessee bears usually den from December through March.

In Florida, some bears may not hibernate at all. Radio signals from an adult male in Florida's Apalachicola National Forest show it did not go into the winter sleep, although it spent several short periods in an inactive state. Immature males have also been known to remain active during the winter in some areas.

The length of hibernation depends more on climate than on any other single factor, but other conditions do affect it, too. In Vermont, for example, black bears will continue feeding right into December if food is plentiful, even though there is snow on the ground; but when food is in short supply, they den before mid-November. Some studies show that adult females den before adult males, perhaps so that the females have a better choice of dens for their cubs. Moreover, dens of females with cubs are often more substantial than those of males, indicating that they may be chosen with more care.

A Minnesota bear and her two cubs, hibernating. (Lynn Rogers)

What does a black bear look for in a den?

First of all, a black bear almost always selects a den that is within its home range. In Minnesota, Lynn Rogers found that male black bears denned not only within their range, but within one small part of it. The den selection, he discovered, was made well in advance of hibernation: when it was time to hibernate, males would move directly to the den, no matter how far from it they were. One male, who had been looking for food outside his range, traveled 104 miles (167 kilometers) to his den; he looked at no other den sites along the way. Rogers thinks the males' den selection probably takes place in the spring, when bears leave their old dens. Females in Rogers's study did not seem to choose their dens so early, and the females' dens were more scattered than the males'.

Smoky Mountains National Park when they received a radio signal from a female bear indicating that she was 30 feet (9 meters) above ground. At first they thought they were misreading the signal, or that the bear had left her radio collar in a tree. But when one of them climbed up the tree from which the signals seemed to be coming, the head of a sleepy bear popped out of a cavity in the trunk 30 feet up. Since then, the researchers have discovered that most female bears in the Smokies den high in large, old trees. The highest entrance they found was 80 feet (24.3 meters) up.

This type of den does not seem to be used in most other areas, although two University of Georgia researchers, Robert J. Hamilton and R. Larry Marchinton, found the tree den of a female bear in North Carolina that had an entrance 81 feet (25 meters) above ground.

Kenneth G. Johnson and his wife, Debra, students of Michael Pelton's at the University of Tennessee, used a computer model to find out why females prefer this kind of den. According to the model, in ground dens in the Smokies, moisture and wind produce a heat loss in the bear's body of 38.34 per cent; in tree dens, the heat loss is only 23.29 per cent. This means a 15.05-per-cent energy saving in tree dens over ground dens. Such a saving means that a female bear using a tree den comes out of hibernation with more fat than a bear using a ground den. During the early spring, when food is scarce, this fat reserve helps the mother and her cubs survive.

Another reason bears choose tree dens probably has to do with safety. Hidden high in a tree, a mother and cubs avoid disturbance from people and other animals. Robert Hamilton found this to be the case with the female denning in the tall North Carolina tree. Previously, she had been denning on the ground in a "Carolina bay," where she was disturbed by a pack of deerhounds. After that she chose to den in the tall, hollow bald-cypress tree in a swamp, where the researchers found her. Hamilton thinks more Carolina bears would den in these trees if more suitable ones were available — many were cut down by loggers, and some of those remaining are hollow to the base and contain water.

No matter where a black-bear den is situated or what its construction, it is usually surprisingly small for such a large animal. One of our party in Pennsylvania, an average-sized man, tried to slip into the rock den formerly used by Yoko, who weighs about 200 pounds (91 kilograms); he got stuck in the entrance. For a master's thesis he wrote at Pennsylvania State University, George Matula measured one Pennsylvania ground den that was 22.4 inches (56 centimeters) deep and 38 inches (94 centimeters) wide at its widest point; the main entrance was 14.4 inches (36 centimeters) by 12 inches (30 centimeters). Tree-cavity dens in the Smokies average 86 inches (218.4 centimeters) high, 23 inches (59.6 centimeters) wide, and 24 inches (62 centimeters) deep; the average entrance is about 15 inches (37.7 centimeters) by 22 inches (55.4 centimeters). Excavated dens in Idaho average 28 inches (71.7 centimeters) high, 42 inches (103.8 centimeters) wide, and 45 inches (111.2 centimeters) deep; their entrances average 17 inches (44.4 centimeters) by 22 inches (57 centimeters).

The Idaho statistics show that adult male bears do

not use bigger dens than female or immature bears, but they do dig somewhat larger entrances, to accommodate their greater size.

The interior of a black-bear den often contains leaves, grass, bark, or branches, which the bear has dragged into the site for bedding. If hay is available, the bear will use that instead. Ground dens are more likely to contain bedding than tree dens, though bears in tree dens in the Smokies often scrape knotted wood off the inside of the tree for bedding. Some studies indicate females with cubs use bedding more than males, but others show both sexes use bedding to the same extent.

All the dens that have been described offer at least some protection, but black bears occasionally choose exposed dens. In Michigan, a female and her three cubs hibernated on top of a muskrat house which consisted of a pile of vegetation. During one of Minnesota's coldest winters, a female, also with three cubs, chose a site at the base of two spindly conifer trees. Maine bears sometimes creep in around the base of a medium-sized balsam fir and let the snow furnish them with their only cover, other than the branches. But in spite of the crudeness of many bear dens, the animals manage to keep warm in them — bears and their cubs seldom die of natural causes in dens.

The way that black bears remain comfortable even in exposed dens has been demonstrated by a unique project carried out by Dr. John F. Craighead, of the University of Montana, and Dr. Frank C. Craighead, Jr., of the State University of New York. They put a radio collar on an adult male black bear in Montana, tracked it to its den, and equipped the den with a number of temperature sensors. Another temperature sensor was put in the bear's rectum. During the winter, signals from the sensors were picked up by a NASA satellite.

The sensors revealed that the hibernating bear creates what the Craigheads call a microclimate around its body. Underneath the bear bed, the average temperature was 65 degrees Fahrenheit (18.1 degrees centigrade), while outdoors the average was only 20 degrees Fahrenheit (−6.7 degrees centigrade). Near the entrance to the den it was almost as cold as it was outside, 27 Fahrenheit (−3.0 centigrade); when the bear left the den, the temperature at the bed also dropped to 27 degrees. The bear's body-temperature readings — picked up for only a short time — ranged from 91 to 95 degrees Fahrenheit (33 to 35 degrees centigrade).

The Craighead experiment indicates that a black bear can effectively keep itself warm in a cold den, although it may have to work harder to do it in some dens than in others. Since the den is cold, the mother bear can keep her cubs warm only if they are next to her body.

Special transmitters that are sensitive to small movements have been attached to bears in hibernation, and they indicate the animals' movements are minimal: bears probably scratch, lick, position their young, and shift their bodies. Movements of this kind have been noted by various observers. Harold Guiher (whose observations of cubs appear in Chapter IV), reports that a mother bear reverses her position in the den every few days. Another observer has described a sleeping mother bear moving her legs and otherwise adjusting her body when her cubs cried.

In spite of their lack of activity in hibernation, black

bears do occasionally leave their dens during the winter. This happens primarily when the animal is disturbed by an intruder. The Idaho study showed that the black bear is most likely to leave its den because of a disturbance in the early part of the denning season, when its body is still not completely adjusted to hibernation. But sometimes a bear will leave its den for what appears to be an exploratory trip, which may take it just a few feet or a longer distance away, before it returns to hibernation. These trips may end with the bear's choosing a new den. One adult female in the Idaho study occupied eight different dens in five winters.

What tells the bear it's time to get up for good? Warming temperatures, melting snow, and longer days all play a part in rousing the black bear in spring. The bear grows restless: observers have seen bears come out of their den, walk around, go back in, then come out again. This behavior may go on for days or even weeks. When the animals finally come out permanently, they go only a short distance from the den, where they construct a nest, or "day bed," for resting and sleeping. The bears stay in the vicinity of the den for a few days, then move on to other parts of their range.

During the period after awakening, bears may eat some food, but they do not seek it as actively as they do later. In any case, little food is available in spring. The bears' remaining fat reserves tide them over until conditions improve.

From this point on, the black bear does not use a den until it goes into hibernation again, in the fall. The day bed, rather than the den, will be where the animal rests and sleeps. Day beds are mounds of vegetation placed in a thicket or other concealed site. Bears build a number of them within their range. Day beds are usually less substantial than dens, although Stephen Herrero found one in Canada's Banff National Park that was 3 to 4 feet (91 to 121 centimeters) across and had walls 18 inches (4.6 centimeters) high. The mother that built it had broken off a 3-inch-thick tree trunk to form a base, and heaped spruce and pine boughs, plants, and grasses on top to make a bed for herself and her cub. It was better constructed than most dens.

CHAPTER VII

The Black Bear and People

One evening in August, about five o'clock, a black bear appeared at Morton Overlook in Great Smoky Mountains National Park. The Overlook is on the Transmountain Road, the only road running through the park, and the bear soon attracted an appreciative audience. Some people stopped their cars and offered it food. Others took photographs. After eating everything that was offered, the bear disappeared into the woods. The next evening, it was back.

When I visited the Smokies that August, the bear had been making regular appearances at Morton Overlook for a week, always about the same time — four to five p.m. Tom Burst, one of Michael Pelton's graduate students at the University of Tennessee, offered to drive me to the Overlook at the appropriate hour to see if the bear would appear.

"It's here, all right," said Burst as we drove up. "Look at all those cars." There were half a dozen parked at the Overlook, and more arriving every minute. At first I couldn't see the bear, but then, as we walked toward the edge of the woods, I made out the dark form against the trees.

It was the first panhandler bear I'd seen and it looked fairly big to me, but Burst said it was a male

A black bear in Great Smoky Mountains National Park gets a handout. (University of Tennessee)

yearling weighing perhaps only 100 to 125 pounds (45 to 56 kilograms).

The bear paced back and forth about twenty feet away. One young man crouched down and held out his hand. The bear came up to him and his companion took a photograph from two feet away. When the animal turned away from the young man, a young woman approached it. She held a child about ten by the hand. Suddenly she scooped up the child in one arm and held a piece of fruit above the bear's head with the other arm. The bear stood up on its hind legs and took the fruit.

"You know, you're not supposed to feed the bears," said Burst to the woman as she was returning to her car.

"Oh, fruit doesn't hurt them," said the woman.

"She thought you didn't want her to feed the bear because it might hurt the bear!" I marveled as we drove off.

But the reason Burst had spoken to her was that feeding bears might hurt *her* — or her child. In the fourteen years between 1964 and 1978, there were 131 injuries caused by black bears in Great Smoky Mountains National Park. Most of them occurred when people were feeding, photographing, or otherwise interacting with bears at close range. There has never been a death in the park caused by a black bear, although there have been a few deaths in other national parks. A visitor was killed by a black bear in Yellowstone National Park in 1947. Canadian parks, which have more black bears than American parks, have more fatalities. In 1978 alone, three people were killed by black bears in Canadian parks.

Although the vast majority of these injuries and deaths are provoked by people who deliberately get too close to the animals, on rare occasions black-bear attacks do not seem to be linked to human carelessness. In 1948 a three-year-old child was dragged off the porch of her house in northern Michigan and killed by a black bear; when the bear was killed, a few days later, no reason could be found for the incident other than the fact that the animal was very thin and had little food in its stomach.

A few other apparently unprovoked incidents have been recorded. In 1976 a woman picking berries in Alberta, Canada, was killed by a black bear. A U.S. Geological Survey geologist on a field trip in Alaska lost both arms to a black bear.

Does this mean the black bear is a dangerous animal that cannot live near people?

Definitely not. Biologists who regularly work with black bears claim the animals are not aggressive, and in fact try to avoid people. When a black bear accidentally meets a human, the bear almost always retreats. "I honestly consider the domestic dog a more serious threat than the black bear," says Gary Alt, of the Pennsylvania Game Commission, who has handled more than 400 bears. The overwhelming number of black-bear incidents, these experts stress, are caused by a few bears that have become habituated to people and frequent areas where food can be found.

In Great Smoky Mountains National Park, Michael Pelton estimates that just five per cent of the black bears cause all the incidents. Research carried out by Pelton and others indicates that the majority of these panhandlers are males, such as the one I saw. One of Pelton's students, however, disagrees. Jane Tate, who wrote her doctoral dissertation on panhandler bears in this park, found that about half the panhandlers were females; in general, the older panhandlers were females, the younger ones males. Tate believes some bears learn panhandling from their mother.

Because they are the most numerous bear in North America and associate more with people, black bears do cause more injuries to humans than other bears. Nevertheless, biologists consider the grizzly bear far more dangerous. Grizzlies are much more likely to attack without provocation. There are at least twenty well-established records of grizzly mothers with cubs attacking hikers in U.S. and Canadian national parks when the hikers suddenly came across the bear family. Black bears, however, as stated earlier, seldom figure in incidents like these.

The Canadian scientist Stephen Herrero believes that black bears evolved into a less dangerous animal than grizzlies because of the blacks' use of trees for protection. A black-bear mother can put her cubs up a tree and climb it herself, if necessary, when threatened.

But a grizzly often lives in relatively treeless terrain, and must defend her cubs and herself on the ground. In the past, the grizzly attack was a successful strategy against enemies like the wolf pack, but when man arrived, this violent defensive behavior gave the animal a reputation as an aggressor. As a result, grizzlies have been exterminated throughout most of their range, while black bears still thrive in many areas.

Even when black bears attack people, the injuries are seldom serious. David Graber, of the University of California, who has studied black bears in Yosemite National Park, describes a typical assault as "a campground bear that loses his temper and takes a swipe at someone, which results in ten to thirty stitches." Ten to thirty stitches is nothing to laugh about, but a black bear is a big, strong animal and it could do far more damage if it wanted to. Jane Tate made films and videotapes of hundreds of encounters between black bears and people for her panhandler-bear study, and what impressed her most about the bears' treatment of people who feed, photograph, and pet the animal is their self-control: "The bears I watched exhibited tremendous restraint — more than I did," she says.

The worst instance of human stupidity around bears that Tate observed was a man who put his baby on the back of a sub-adult male about the size of the one I had seen — 100 to 125 pounds. The bear did nothing. Another time, Tate saw a man put honey on his hand and let a bear lick it off. Again, nothing happened. She has slides of a number of people even putting their hands inside the mouths of bears to feed them; in most cases, no aggression occurred on the part of the bears.

In the majority of cases in which a bear did show

aggression, the act that brought it on was the person getting too close to the bear. In one incident, a teen-aged girl passed near an adult male bear. The bear appeared disturbed to Tate, but the girl, not realizing this, walked closer to the animal. Suddenly the bear charged the girl, stopped, and *rested* its teeth on her upper leg. The girl was not hurt.

Such restraint is shown by black bears even when they are injuring people. Three young boys Tate watched kept hitting a large female bear that was looking for food in a campground. She made a number of threatening sounds for about fifteen minutes. When this produced no results, she knocked one of the youngsters to the ground and nipped him on the back of the neck and the back, as if he were her cub. Then she walked away, veered toward Tate ("I was being warned," she says), and left the campground.

Tate and her assistants had begun shouting when the boy was knocked down and the boy's mother strolled over as the bear was leaving. She helped her son to his feet — and then walked off. The boy's injuries were negligible.

Tate's research indicates that bears, like the female just described, usually give warning signs of aggression, which humans can read if they're smart enough. "I feel I can pretty much predict what bears are going to do," says Tate. In her dissertation, she used a classification of aggressive sounds and actions worked out by Cheryl Pruitt, another of Burghardt's students. Tate ranks these sounds and actions from mild to serious.

The mildest signs of aggression that a bear gives are sounds: low moans, a blowing sound (sometimes called woofing), and "jaw popping," a hollow noise made by the bear with its lips and jaw. If none of this has any effect, a bear may run toward the annoying person or group, its head in the same plane as its body; its ears are not flattened. Sometimes the bear blows — woofs — while it is running.

If the bear still feels threatened after going through the first part of its aggressive repertoire, it will intensify its warnings. It will now swat with its paws while standing either on its two back legs or on all fours. The swats may be directed toward either a person or an object, and they, too, may be accompanied by blowing. A charge is a still more serious form of aggression. In a charge, as distinguished from simply running toward a person, the bear lowers its head and flattens its ears.

The last and most serious aggressive action a bear takes is actually snapping or biting, or forcing the person to the ground with the forepaws. Sometimes the bear uses its claws, too.

If a black bear begins making aggressive sounds and motions, take care. Stop whatever you are doing that is annoying the animal and slowly retreat. An escalation in the bear's aggression can usually be halted by your realizing that what the animal is trying to say is: Keep away! It is thought, in fact, that among bears these same aggressive sounds and actions keep fights to a minimum.

In the unlikely event that a black bear continues its aggression until it actually charges you, don't panic. Researchers who have faced black-bear charges say most of them are bluffs. The best thing to do if this happens, believes Michael Pelton, is to stand still or slowly move away. If the bear's aggression persists, shout, or throw stones or sticks at it. Pelton once stopped a bear charging a photographer by throwing a stone at the animal.

Another researcher, Carole Jorgensen — who wrote her master's thesis at the University of Montana on bear-livestock interactions — advocates packing a loaded water pistol when in bear country. If a bear acts aggressive, she counsels, squirt it in the face. "Bears are bluffers and we have to bluff, too," she says.

Human injuries and deaths caused by black bears get most of the publicity, but the vast majority of problems associated with these animals involve damage to property, not people. Black bears have been responsible for everything from ripping up backpacks to upturning beehives. As with human injuries from panhandling bears, almost all bear damage derives ultimately from the animal's ravenous appetite. Researchers in many areas of the country can point to a clear increase in incidents when there is a shortage of wild foods.

The most serious property damage occurs in Washington State, where bears harm the trees on which the logging industry is based. Their main target is the Douglas fir, but they also like western hemlock and western red cedar, among other species. Tree damage by bears also occurs in Oregon and a few other states.

Richard J. Poelker, of the Washington State Game Department, and Harry D. Hartwell, of the Department of Natural Resources, have discovered that black bears damage trees by peeling off strips of bark to get at the sapwood underneath; they eat the sapwood for the sugar. Usually the damage is around the bottom of the tree, but sometimes bears climb as high as fifty feet to pull off bark. If the bark is torn off all the way around the tree, the tree dies. Most trees have only part of their bark removed, but then they are subject to fungus infections that can damage the wood.

To combat this problem, Washington timber companies hire professional hunters to kill black bears with special permits issued by the state. (One of these hunters, Jack Aldrich, invented the Aldrich foot snare — described in Chapter I — now used by bear biologists throughout the United States.) The professional hunters currently operate only in areas of western Washington where black bears cause extensive damage. A special spring hunting season takes place in these same areas. Between professional and amateur hunters, both the number of bears in the area and the amount of damage have been reduced.

Another common form of property damage caused

Red cedar tree stripped of bark by black bears. The marks were made by bears' teeth. (Rich Poelker, Washington Department of Game)

by black bears is the destruction of beehives to get honey and young bees. Although this isn't as serious as tree damage, it is more widespread. In the early summer of 1979, a bear tore up some beehives in a town twenty miles from my house, in western New Jersey, a state with very few black bears. The animal was seen by the owner of the hives, who said it probably weighed about 100 pounds (45 kilograms). This size and the time of year indicated that the bear was probably a yearling about one and a half years old. It was undoubtedly just passing through the area, as the only suitable habitat for bears in New Jersey is the extreme northwestern corner.

Bear damage to beehives in New Jersey is rare, but it is a real concern in such states as Georgia, Florida, and North and South Carolina. In South Carolina in 1977, beehive losses to bears totaled 32,000 dollars. Beekeepers may legally kill bears in most states where bears damage beehives. In Florida during some years, more bears have been killed by beekeepers than by hunters during the bear season (bear hunting in Florida is confined to only a few areas).

State biologists encourage methods of bear control around beehives that do not include killing the bears. So far, the most successful methods seem to be electric fences and raised platforms for the hives. Another promising method of control, which is still being tested, is aversive conditioning. This is a process in which an animal undergoes a painful experience when it performs a certain act. The animal thus links the act with the pain, so that it stops performing the act — or so the theory goes, at any rate.

Canadian researchers Michael J. Dorrance and John

R. Gunson captured bears raiding beehives in Alberta, Canada — where beehive damage is a big problem — and gave the bears either a series of electric shocks or honey mixed with a substance that made the animals sick. Then they released the bears. The researchers tracked the radio-collared animals for an entire summer and found that most of them did not get into any more beehives. This indicates that aversive conditioning may prevent some forms of property damage by bears.

Crop damage, like beehive damage, is an old story with black bears. Records dating back to the seventeenth century in New England describe bears raiding farmers' fields. Today, however, crop raiding by bears in most places is a minor problem, although on particular farms it can be severe. In the area bordering Shenandoah National Park, in Virginia, black bears sometimes knock down as much as a half acre of corn as they move through a field. Bears' favorite crops are the same as 300 years ago: corn, wheat, oats, and apples.

Although black bears are primarily vegetarians, they occasionally eat livestock, as well as wild animals. Surveys of livestock killings in fifteen Western states demonstrate that black bears account for a small percentage of the losses. Bears are most likely to kill both livestock and wild game in the spring, when other food is scarce, and the animal bears are most likely to kill is the sheep. Calves, goats, hogs, chickens, turkeys, and even fish are also taken. Livestock owners in some states can receive payments for losses due to animals, including bears. One survey shows, however, that in Colorado most claims of killings by bears were unjustified: bears were often assumed to have killed live-stock when they were simply feeding on animals that had died of other causes.

Nevertheless, bears definitely do kill animals. Carole Jorgensen's research shows that when a bear kills another animal of any size, it usually does so by biting it on the back of the neck and the spine. It may also claw the back and chest, and bite other parts of the body. Some bears strike their prey with the forepaw. A researcher who investigated killings by bears in Maine believes that bears bite other animals if there is only one victim involved, but that if there is more than one, the bear uses forepaw blows. In a case in which a bear killed a number of cattle, it was found that all had died of a broken neck, and they had bruises and claw marks around the head and neck.

After a bear kills a large domestic animal, it usually drags it to a secluded area for feeding. The bear eats the whole carcass in one sitting if undisturbed; otherwise, it will leave the animal and then come back for a day or two. Occasionally, a bear will bury a carcass, much as a dog does.

Examinations of bear stomachs and scats show that the wild animals bears sometimes eat include rabbits, mice, birds, squirrels, woodchucks, beaver, and opossum. They also eat larger animals, but bears usually confine themselves to the young of these species, or to trapped animals. Among the larger species eaten are white-tailed deer and their fawns, and elk and moose calves. In addition, there are several cases on record of black bears' attacking and eating other black bears, in traps, and of males' eating cubs.

Nevertheless, the incidence of black-bear predation

on game animals is not high, although there are some exceptions. Biologist Mike Schlegel, of the Idaho Fish and Game Department, found that sixty-five per cent of the elk calves born in one part of the state were being killed by black bears. Another member of the department, John Beecham, directed a program to transport black bears out of this area, to see if the extent of the predation could be reduced. There is some evidence that in Alaska moose calves are heavily preyed on by black bears.

Black-bear predation of wild and domestic animals, and damage to specialized industries, isn't of much concern to most Americans, but a new kind of property damage by bears is affecting more and more of us. A 1976 study by Dale Harms, of the National Park Service, shows that in the national parks the rate of damage to visitors' property by bears — principally black bears — is rising. (By contrast, the rate of injuries to people is falling.) Most of this damage, Harms found, occurs in just four parks: Great Smoky Mountains, Shenandoah, California's Sequoia-Kings Canyon (actually two adjoining parks), and Yosemite.

Yosemite, whose bears are only blacks, had almost half the total park-damage incidents recorded in the country in 1976. The biggest problem involves cars. One Porsche sustained 3000 dollars' worth of damage from a bear that tore it up looking for food.

Yosemite is a 1100-square-mile park located about four hours from San Francisco in the rugged Sierra Nevada. It was one of the first national parks created, and now attracts close to three million visitors a year. In the last decade, more and more of its visitors have been backpackers who hike into the backcountry, where most of Yosemite's 300 black bears live. As a result, black-bear property damage in the backcountry is rising; in 1979, there were an estimated 2800 bear incidents in Yosemite's backcountry, amounting to 56,250 dollars in damages.

Backcountry bear incidents are also increasing in other parks with black bears, a trend that concerns bear experts. Frontcountry bears, the traditional panhandlers, often seem to know how to behave around people, but backcountry bears can be impolite, to say the least. Researcher Ellis Bacon (see Chapter II) lived in a cottage near the Appalachian Trail in Great Smoky Mountains National Park one summer. On a Sunday afternoon, he heard something that sounded like a football game from the direction of a shelter along the Trail — there were shouts and the clanging of metal. When he went to investigate, he found that two backcountry bears had chased all the hikers up on top of the shelter so that the bears could get the hikers' food. The hikers were trying to drive the bears away by yelling and beating pots and pans together.

Shortly after this incident, the park required overnight hikers along the Appalachian Trail to get a shelter-use permit, which restricts the number of persons at any one shelter. Since then, the bear problem along the Trail has decreased. But property damage continues to increase in other areas of the park's backcountry, along with the number of backpackers. Michael Pelton believes that the backcountry trails in this park are overused. In the future, he predicts, some restrictions will have to be put on the number of backpackers and the trails they may use.

The backcountry bear problem, like the frontcountry

bear problem, is basically caused by people either feeding the bears or failing to store food properly. But, as the Harms study makes clear, you yourself do not have to feed a bear or leave food around to be bothered by a panhandler. A few experiences of being fed or finding carelessly stored food quickly conditions bears to make a connection between food and people. Once that happens, at least a few bears will look for food even around people who do not feed them and who store food properly. Almost seventy-five per cent of the backcountry bears that caused property damage in Harms's study proved to have been conditioned this way.

Frontcountry bears can be conditioned, too, but controls over people are easier to enforce in the frontcountry than the backcountry. "You can't follow millions of people around," as Ellis Bacon puts it.

Nevertheless, Yosemite has recently instituted stringent measures against the encouragement of bear panhandling in all parts of the park, and the program seems to be working. While property damage by bears in the backcountry continues to increase, it has gone down in the park as a whole, and the number of injuries to people has plummeted. Even in the backcountry, the number of incidents per visitor has decreased, although the total number of incidents has risen, because there are more visitors.

When you visit Yosemite today, you receive a brochure telling you about the dangers of feeding bears, and that the practice in the park is strictly prohibited. Signs throughout the park give the same message. In addition, a new federal regulation requires campers to store food properly. If you have a car, you must keep food in the trunk or, if you have no trunk, out of sight under the seat. If you are backpacking, you have to string your food up on a wire between two trees; cables for this purpose are furnished in many backcountry campsites. In 1980 slide programs and displays were set up at visitor centers to demonstrate proper methods of storing food in the park. The future may bring a limitation on the number of visitors in certain backcountry areas.

For its part, Yosemite has closed all its open garbage dumps and "bear-proofed" its garbage cans, so bears can't get into them. Food lockers are being installed in campgrounds accessible to cars. When a bear does cause injury or property damage, the animal is promptly removed from the trouble spot and relocated some distance away. However, as Yosemite is not a big national park, many relocated bears return to the

Some black bears in Yosemite National Park have learned how to reach food hung high off the ground. (David Graber)

scene of the crime — forty-nine per cent of bears moved in 1975 had returned two years later. When a problem bear persists in returning and causing trouble, it is killed. Eight bears were killed in Yosemite in 1979 after a careful review of their records.

The overall drop in bear-caused injuries and front-country property damage indicates that the Yosemite program is working. But there is another sign of success. David Graber made a study of bear scats in 1976, a year after the program went into effect, and he found that bears in Yosemite Valley, the park's most popular area, ate far less artificial food than they had done before the program started. Eventually, as bears are forced to depend more and more on wild foods, their population is expected to decline — the population is believed to have been only about 125 in 1924, before much food was brought in by visitors. A monitoring system is being set up by the park to make sure bear mortality is not excessive.

A strict bear-control program can be successful in a popular park, as the example of Yellowstone National Park shows. Located in Montana, Idaho, and Wyoming, Yellowstone used to have one of the worst black-bear injury and property-damage records among the parks: in the thirty years before 1970, there was an average of forty-six injuries a year, some of which required hospitalization. In 1947 a death occurred.

As with some other parks, Yellowstone's managers were partly responsible for the problem. When my husband worked there one summer in the 1950s, he saw black bears feeding in the evenings in an open dump located between a large lodge and a campground; to encourage visitors to watch the nightly "show," the

Handouts were common in Yellowstone National Park before controls were put into effect. (National Park Service)

park had set up bleachers at the edge of the dump and the area was spotlighted.

The bleachers, lights, and open dumps are all gone today, along with the park's encouragement of bear feeding. Not only did Yellowstone close all its open dumps, but also it fenced in its landfill sites and incinerators, and bear-proofed its garbage cans. Once common along the park's roads, black bears today are hard to see, because most of them are in the backcountry. In 1976, Yellowstone had one of the lowest injury and property damage rates of the national parks, although it has more black bears — about 650 — than any park outside Alaska.

The two Eastern national parks with large numbers of black bears, Great Smoky Mountains and Shenandoah, are also taking measures to control bear problems. Both parks have bear-proofed garbage cans, and they remove problem animals to remote sections of the park. Campers are required to seal food in a vehicle or suspend it from a tree at least 10 feet (3 meters) from the ground in campgrounds. When I visited Great Smoky Mountains National Park in 1979, the park was putting in 18-foot (5.5-meter) metal poles at backcountry campsites, from which campers could hang their food.

Unfortunately, even the best preventive measures don't work at 100-per-cent efficiency, thanks to the cleverness of black bears. In Great Smoky Mountains National Park, a few bears shinny up the food poles. Yosemite's backcountry bears include some inventive animals that use various means of manipulating the cable-and-pulley system so that the suspended food either drops or can be reached by the bear. Frontcountry bears are ingenious, too: after food in their area was required to be stored in car trunks, some bears began breaking into cars and tearing out the back seat to reach the trunk.

But technology may yet outwit the black bear. Bruce Hastings, of Utah State University, who has been studying black bears in Western national parks, recently discovered that the animals are unable to break into containers made from PVC (polyvinyl chloride) pipe. His finding indicates that park visitors may be able to stuff their food inside light, inexpensive PVC containers that can fit inside a backpack. The containers have been tested at Yosemite and look very promising.

Since all bear incidents revolve around food, directly

A black bear that has been conditioned to expect food from people may help itself boldly, like this one in Great Smoky Mountains National Park. (University of Tennessee)

or indirectly, Michael Pelton has recently developed a list of nine rules for taking food into national parks or other areas with black bears.

1. Store all food in your car trunk when camping with a vehicle.
2. Try to cut down on the amount of food opened but not eaten.
3. When in the backcountry, burn all garbage and carry residue, such as cans, out of the area. In campgrounds, place garbage in proper receptacles.
4. Take no food into a tent or sleeping bag.
5. Store articles for carrying or cooking food out of sight.

6. In backcountry areas, hang all food in a bag suspended on a rope between two trees. The bag should be at least 8 feet from the ground.

7. Try putting mothballs in your backpack or near food containers, to mask the scent of food.

8. If a bear does move toward a pack or other item, shout or throw rocks or sticks at it.

9. Give bears a wide berth.

David Graber adds another rule, for cases in which a black bear approaches you while you are actually eating or cooking: quickly gather up everything edible and back off steadily. Yell and toss rocks in the unlikely event the bear follows you.

Another way in which our national parks are handling bear problems is by means of BIMS, the Bear Information Management System. In 1978 six parks with a high number of bear incidents set up a joint computer program to store data on bear observations, incidents, and management actions. The parks enter information into the system as often as they want, by means of computer terminals at the individual parks. At Yosemite, for instance, detailed information on bear incidents and captures for relocation is entered into BIMS for each problem bear. These data are retrieved whenever a decision has to be made on killing a problem bear.

Yet in spite of the trouble bears sometimes cause, most people who visit parks want the animals there. Every survey that has ever been taken in Yosemite shows that visitors to the park rank black bears among its leading attractions.

A recent survey taken in Great Smoky Mountains

National Park — by Michael Pelton, Charles D. Scott, of the Tennessee Wildlife Resources Agency, and Gordon Burghardt — covered only those people who had either been injured by or had property damaged by a bear. Of these people, all but one thought bears should remain in the park. Some were indignant at even being asked if bears should stay. "They were here first, we are the intruders," said one person. Not only that, but sixty-four per cent of those who participated in the survey thought bears were not a serious problem. Almost half took full responsibility for the bear incident in which they had been involved.

lack bear left in the author's area of New Jersey is this
from a thirty-foot-high tree.

CHAPTER VIII

Can People Live with Black Bears?

"I know black bears can live with people," said ologist Gary Alt, of the Pennsylvania Game Com sion, at a recent bear conference. "But can peopl with bears?"

The question sums up the black bear's pros North America. The black bear is an adapt persistent animal, capable of living in a wide habitats. It can also live close to people eastern Pennsylvania, where Alt works, b being born right inside vacation-house This century has even seen the black be est comeback in several states from w absent in the East. But the dwir black bears in many other areas i point beyond which even the bear

Black bears are still very plen the United States. Alaska, Id Oregon all have populations a either stable or increasing. have very sizable populatio nia's may be decreasing. S eastern half, including M Wisconsin, and Minne

The only b
one carved

bears; in all these states, the population is believed to be stable or increasing.

Some other states have smaller though still sizable populations. Arkansas has 1200 to 1500, Arizona from 2000 to 3500, North Carolina about 2000 (including those in Great Smoky Mountains National Park), Pennsylvania 2000 to 3500, Vermont about 1500, Virginia from 1000 to 1500 (including those in Shenandoah National Park).

Where the black bear is in trouble today is outside the protected areas in much of the eastern half of the United States. Many Eastern and Middle Western states have no black bears at all, or fewer than 100. States with fewer than 500 include Alabama, Florida, Georgia, Tennessee (outside Great Smoky Mountains National Park), and Louisiana. West Virginia has about 650. These numbers are too low to put the black bear in the safe category in any of these states. The animal may also be in a decline in states with larger bear populations, such as Pennsylvania and Virginia.

Most of the states with a low or declining black-bear population are making efforts to stabilize or increase the number of bears, and there are signs of success. Georgia has only a few hundred bears, but the number is believed to have increased recently. North Carolina's bear population may have increased recently, too, partly because of a new system of sanctuaries in which bears are protected. But unless the underlying conditions that have brought about the bear's decline are changed, any improvement may be short-lived.

The reason for the decline in black bears is the same in all states: pressures of various kinds from an expanding human population.

Northeastern Pennsylvania was once an area of hilly forests, berry-filled swamps, and small to medium-sized farms. Black bears were very common. Today the area is still largely rural, but it has many vacation houses and other tourist-oriented development. New highways bring in thousands of visitors from the urbanized parts of Pennsylvania, New York, and New Jersey. Black bears remain numerous but they are being subjected to increasing pressures as the human population rises. Not only are the animals being killed on highways (eighty-four killed in one recent year), but they are also being forced to share their habitat with people.

Gary Alt and other members of the Pennsylvania Game Commission are frequently called upon to remove bears that are causing problems in what was once bear habitat. The animals are guilty of the usual bear mischief: tearing off porch screens to get food, destroying bird feeders, upsetting garbage cans. There are few injuries to humans and all those Alt investigated were provoked by someone petting or hand-feeding a bear. Many calls come from urban dwellers who have simply *seen* a bear that (to eyes unused to bears) looks menacing.

Another pressure faced by black bears in northeastern Pennsylvania is heavy hunting. Until the 1970s, hunters killed too few bears to affect the population structure; each year, enough cubs were born to offset the number of animals killed by hunters. But between 1972 and 1976, the number of hunters more than doubled. The number of bears killed by hunters increased, too, even though the hunting season was only one day long. In 1977 and 1978, the bear-hunting season was closed,

and there was a marked increase in bears. Dr. James
S. Lindzey, of the Pennsylvania Cooperative Wildlife Research Unit, who has directed many bear-research
projects in the state, thinks bears will remain in Pennsylvania but in lower numbers than existed in the 1940s.

What is happening in northeastern Pennsylvania is
also happening in other parts of the eastern United
States that retain a black-bear population. In some
areas, the pressure comes from the construction of vacation houses, in others from industry and large-scale
agriculture. Vermont, like Pennsylvania, has experi-
enced a boom in vacation houses, most of them built
on former bear habitat. In coastal North Carolina,
large corporate farms are replacing swamps that once
sheltered numerous bears. Florida is the scene of large-
scale logging operations that drain swamps and re-
place them with pine "plantations" — acre after acre
of the same species of pine.

Although bears are subject to the most intense
human pressure in the eastern United States, the same
kind of pressure occurs in the West. In northern California, which has a large logging industry, some logging practices both reduce the amount of bear food and
make the bear habitat easier for people to reach.
Hunters thus kill more bears in the areas opened up by
logging, a trend that may play a part in the decline in
California's black-bear population.

In the future, the pressures on black bears are going
to increase everywhere in the United States. The
human population of our country is now about
220,000,000. The U.S. Bureau of the Census projects
that by the year 2050, we will have 315,622,000 people,
almost 100 million more than we do today. This large

increase in the human population in less than a century is bound to affect all our wildlife, even in areas where it is now plentiful.

Can the black bear survive in an era of reduced bear habitat and more people? Or, as Gary Alt asks, can people live with bears?

The question is debated at conferences on bears and in wildlife publications. Black bears and most other large wild animals, experts agree, will probably survive in some protected areas, such as parks and refuges. Thanks to the foresight of conservationists, the United States has some 778 million acres (311 million hectares) of public land, most of it owned by the federal government. This land will remain largely undeveloped, though energy exploration will affect some parts of it, as will the growing number of campers and

As the number of park visitors increases, bears become more and more threatened. Michael Pelton holds the skull of a bear killed on the road in Great Smoky Mountains National Park.

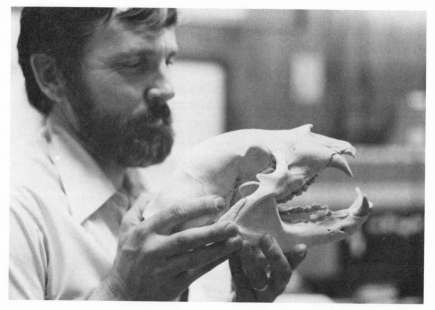

others visiting our parks and wildlife refuges. The rising number of bear incidents in Yosemite and other parks shows what happens when too many people intrude on bear habitat.

Today, however, most wildlife in the United States, including black bears, still lives on privately owned land. It is here that the black bear's existence is in question. Although some private lands are not suitable for development, even remote private areas will probably feel the impact of the search for energy resources to supply our growing population.

If the black bear is to continue to exist in most of the areas it is found today, it will depend, not on the bear's ability to survive, but on us. We can ensure the black bear's future.

One basic way we can help the black bear survive is by adopting a realistic attitude toward the animal. In the United States, one of three unrealistic attitudes toward the black bear characterizes the thinking of many people. Some look on all bears, but particularly the black bear, as a sort of toy to be petted, fed, and photographed. Others think of all bears as monsters that eat people. A third group sees black bears as the enemy, to be combated: "The only good bear is a dead bear" is the attitude of this group.

Such attitudes often have deep roots, making them hard to overcome. In the early days of white settlement in America, grizzlies and black bears frequently ate farmers' crops and killed an occasional sheep, pig, or calf. Today, predation by bears is only a minor problem, but the old attitudes toward the animal linger on, particularly in areas with an agricultural tradition. Poaching — illegal killing — of black bears is such a serious problem in some parts of the United States that it keeps the animal's population below the level at which it can remain stable, or else eliminates the animal completely. The Virginia Wildlife Federation recently offered a reward of 1000 dollars for information leading to the arrest and conviction of any person killing a bear illegally in the state.

Poaching even takes place in protected areas. It is estimated that every year 80 to 100 black bears are killed illegally by poachers in and adjacent to Great Smoky Mountains National Park.

While people in rural areas sometimes regard black bears with hostility, people in urban areas tend to look on them with pure terror. In New Jersey and Massachusetts, both largely urban, state wildlife personnel are sometimes called on to capture a wandering black bear, only to find it has been shot by the police at the urging of panicked residents. In one Massachusetts town, the fire department sprayed a mother bear and her cubs with fire hoses as they clung to a tree. Only when wildlife officers arrived were the soaked bears allowed to escape.

Most of the bears that turn up in urban and suburban areas are males less than three years old. Bears this age often wander far from home, looking for a range in which to establish themselves. Not aware that bear habitat is limited in most places, these animals may travel through towns and subdivisions in their search. Scientists who work regularly with black bears tell us such wandering bears are seldom dangerous. The best thing to do if you see a bear in an urban or suburban setting is nothing. Don't feed it. Just enjoy watching it and let it go on its way.

If the animal stays around, or is engaged in some kind of property damage, telephone your state wildlife department (some of these are known as departments of environmental protection or conservation). Every state with bears has experts who will remove problem animals to a more suitable location.

Sometimes urban "bear incidents" have their funny aspects. One night Kent Kammermeyer, a wildlife biologist with the state of Georgia, was called to an area near Lake Sidney Lanier to remove what was described as "a thirty-pound bear cub." As he drove to the site, Kammermeyer worried about the whereabouts of the bear's mother, who would undoubtedly stay close to a cub of this size. When he arrived at the scene, he found two deputy sheriffs, three firemen, and a dozen local residents, all peering up a tall pine tree.

One of the deputies pointed his flashlight at the tree. "There he is!" he cried. Kammermeyer looked upward and heaved a sigh of relief. The "bear cub" was a groundhog that had been treed by dogs. It weighed eight pounds.

Curiously enough, the same animal that arouses terror and hostility in some Americans arouses very different feelings in others. Some people seem to regard bears as outsize furry toys. Panhandler bears in national parks are particularly likely to bring out these sentiments. When Jane Tate was doing her study of panhandlers in Great Smoky Mountains National Park, she watched hundreds of encounters between visitors and bears, and concluded there is a "primal urge" on the part of many people to touch the animals. One elderly woman insisted that the panhandlers had been trained by the park rangers to meet people (the bears were kept in a special cage near the Visitors' Center to undergo their "training," the woman informed Tate).

Why do some Americans behave so foolishly around a potentially dangerous animal?

Gordon Burghardt's and Michael Pelton's survey of the attitudes of visitors at Great Smoky Mountains National Park indicates that, although visitors are warned of the dangers of feeding and petting bears, the information is often disregarded. Pelton believes it is because of people's early exposure to a different concept of bears. He mentions teddy bears; fairy tales such as "Goldilocks and the Three Bears"; the symbol of the U.S. Forest Service, Smokey the Bear; and bears portrayed on television and in films. All paint a picture of a humanized bear.

For example, when I was doing research for this book, I saw a new feature film aimed at young people. The plot concerned a family with several children living in a small cabin in the remote wilderness. Among their household pets were a full-grown female black bear and her two cubs. The bears lived in the cabin with the family, behaving like dogs. The film bears, of course, had been carefully trained for their performance; black bears, even ones that are used to people, simply don't behave this way. It's very difficult to keep very young cubs in the house, let alone adult bears, as several scientists can attest.

Probably nothing has done more to present a false image of the bear than the lovable teddy bear. There is a good chance that the original bear on which the teddy is based was a black bear.

In 1902 Theodore (Teddy) Roosevelt, who was then president of the United States, was in Mississippi to

A bear sitting up or standing on its hind legs seems more like a
person than an animal. (National Park Service)

settle a boundary dispute between that state and Louisiana. While there, he took time out to indulge in his favorite hobby, hunting. His party came across a small black bear cub — Mississippi then had a high number of black bears — but Roosevelt refused to shoot it because of its size. The incident was publicized in a newspaper cartoon, inspiring a Brooklyn toy maker, Morris Michtom, to make up a small bear and offer it for sale next to a copy of the cartoon. He called it "Teddy's bear." It sold well and Michtom formed a partnership with a toy wholesaler to market the bear. About the same time, a German firm had begun selling a toy bear, and it, too, was known as the teddy bear. Before long, many U.S. and German firms were selling teddy bears, and they became one of the most popular toys ever made.

We don't have to get rid of teddy bears, but an awareness of how false concepts of the bear affect us may help save the real black bear. Michael Pelton speculates that when people who know only teddy bears, trained movie bears, and fairy-tale bears see real bears standing on their hind legs, begging, the animals seem to them more like people than animals. As a result, they treat the panhandling bears in parks like humans, or at least tame pets, when they are really wild animals. The solution, believes Pelton, is not to provide more information on bears in national parks (the parks already do a good job of informing visitors), but rather to provide a deeper educational process that begins in school. "The Park Service alone cannot be expected to completely reorient a visitor's thinking during his brief stay in the park," Pelton says.

It's difficult to say which of the wrong attitudes toward bears is the most dangerous to the animal (as well as to people). Hostility and fear often result in dead bears, but so does the urge to get close to bears. Bears that have been habituated to human food by well-meaning people usually become pests, and sooner or later they must be transported to a different area. In some cases, the bear manages to adapt to its new home, but in many cases it is killed (legally or illegally), or else it homes to the site where it panhandled in the past. Most persistent homers eventually have to be destroyed.

"If you feed a bear, you are essentially signing a death warrant for that bear if it becomes a depredation problem," says Carole Jorgensen.

Our attitudes toward the black bear will play an important part in the animal's future, but the single most important factor in its survival is habitat. Without proper bear habitat, even the most enlightened attitudes and sophisticated management will be useless. Intrusion into bear habitat by land development is inevitable in a growing nation, but many bear experts believe development can be controlled so that people and bears can continue to live together. Black bears are adaptable, the experts emphasize. Although they thrive in wilderness, if we provide them with the food, cover, and denning sites they need, the animals can also live in areas we use for our own purposes.

Logging is a case in point. One of the major uses of bear habitat, logging can be carried out in a way that actually benefits black bears and other large forest animals, such as elk. Bears feed mainly in understory vegetation found in forest clearings and at forest edges. By cutting all the timber in small areas, logging creates clearings, or "clearcuts," where bear foods grow, permitting more bears to live in the area, and resulting in higher reproductive rates among these animals. Selective cutting — the cutting of individual mature trees — has an even more beneficial effect on understory growth and bear habitat. In Pennsylvania, I saw a bear hibernating beneath a pile of brush created by a small selective cut on land owned by a public utility.

But many logging practices have a detrimental effect on bears. If there are too many clearcuts, and they are too large, bears fear to venture out into them from the safety of the forest. Destruction of the underbrush in clearings by machines or chemicals, in order to encourage the growth of timber, destroys bear foods. Planting large areas with one kind of tree, such as pines, reduces the variety of foods. The cutting down of large old trees used for dens by females drives bears away, or else reduces their chances of survival.

The U.S. Forest Service, which is part of the Department of Agriculture, owns some of the forests that serve as black-bear habitat in both the eastern and the western United States. Logging, mineral exploration, and other uses of these forests are either leased or sold to individuals and industry, but federal laws require the Forest Service to manage the lands so as to preserve the wildlife. Despite such protective management, however, the many uses to which these lands are put sometimes make it difficult to consider the black bear's particular needs.

In some states, the state's bear biologists now participate in decisions made by the Forest Service on the management of its lands. Every winter, personnel from the Tennessee Wildlife Resources Agency meet with the local Forest Service personnel in their area to discuss the Service's projects for the coming year. In one recent session, the Agency and the University of Tennessee informed the Forest Service that large old trees with natural cavities are needed by female bears for dens, and the Forest Service agreed to save the trees from logging.

This kind of cooperation on public lands will probably increase in the future, but it is harder for bear experts to participate in the decisions made by private lumber companies, which control much of the bear habitat in the United States. These companies often do consider wildlife in their plans, but their primary motive is profit, and logging methods that benefit bears are not as profitable as other methods. Eventually, some type of legislation may be necessary to enforce land management on private lands that will benefit black bears and other wildlife.

Most Americans support controls on logging that help wildlife, according to a recent survey of 3,107 people in all areas of the country, taken by Dr. Stephen Kellert, of Yale University. The survey revealed that seventy-six per cent believe logging should be done in ways that benefit the animals even if it results in higher lumber prices.

If it is hard for biologists and other bear experts to influence private timber companies, it is even harder for them to influence the government bodies that control the development of land for housing, industry, highways, and other purposes. In the past, the welfare of black bears and other wildlife has not been considered in most decisions on land use. If we want black bears to remain part of our environment, we will have to demand that their needs be respected. Areas such as the banks of streams and ponds — heavily used by bears for food in spring and summer — may have to be ruled out for development.

Controls will probably also have to be put on human activities in remote sections of parks, national forests, and other public lands with bear populations. A committee of bear experts recently suggested a new status for these areas: the bear zone. A bear zone would be an area with a heavy bear population in which bears, not humans, would be given priority. Once a bear zone is declared, people entering it for any activity would be provided with rules for conduct and suggestions on how to meet them. After that, they would have to be prepared to accept what the committee calls a "reasonable risk." "It seems reasonable," said the committee, "that humans should modify their actions in some areas to insure the continued presence of bears."

One promising movement that has developed with regard to black-bear habitat in the eastern United States is the creation of bear sanctuaries. North Carolina, Tennessee, and West Virginia, all of which have had problems maintaining their black-bear population, have set up large areas of good bear habitat in which the animals may not be hunted. The theory behind the sanctuary is that it encourages an existing population to breed. The excess bears (mostly young males) then leave the sanctuary and move to areas where they may be hunted legally.

North Carolina has twenty-six bear sanctuaries, Tennessee four, and West Virginia two. About three-quarters of a million acres (300,000 hectares) in North Carolina alone have been devoted to its sanctuaries.

The Daniel Boone Bear Sanctuary near Morganton, North Carolina, includes 44,000 acres. In the background is Hawksbill Mountain. (John M. Collins, North Carolina Wildlife Resources Commission)

Some are large, including one that includes 85,000 acres (34,000 hectares).

The sanctuary concept isn't really new, as North Carolina wildlife biologist John M. Collins points out. National parks and wildlife refuges serve as sanctuaries for some animals, playing an important part in preserving these species. Two national parks in the East, Great Smoky Mountains and Shenandoah, serve as sanctuaries for black bears; without the "leakage" of bears from these two parks, the animal's population in the surrounding areas would probably have dropped more than it has.

The sanctuary system is still too new to say if it is successful, though there are some encouraging signs in North Carolina and Tennessee. In North Carolina, which set up its first bear sanctuary in 1971, the former decline in bear numbers has apparently been reversed. In Tennessee sanctuaries, all of which are in the Cherokee National Forest, observations of bears have increased since the sanctuaries were established, in 1973. A recent capture program in one Tennessee sanctuary demonstrated that the bear density was, indeed, higher than it had been. In this sanctuary, according to Richard H. Conley, of the Tennessee Wildlife Resources Agency, the density is estimated to be one bear per square mile (2.6 square meters), more than twice that of the state as a whole.

We still need to know much more about bear habitat, however, before our efforts for bears can be successful. How much variety in foods do black bears need? If there is enough natural food in an area, will bears prey on livestock? How important is water? Are certain kinds of den sites vital to breeding? How much cover do black bears need to insure a stable population? Will the construction of one vacation house drive bears out, or does it take two, ten, or more? What will be the effect of a new road in black-bear habitat?

Research will eventually provide the answers. When it does, black-bear experts hope to be able to sit down with land managers and tell them, with the aid of maps and other graphic materials, exactly how a certain land use will affect a resident population of black bears.

One way in which bear researchers and managers are making black-bear information available today is through a new international organization, the Bear Biology Association. Since 1968 it has held five international conferences. Presentations on black-bear research and management have been an important part of every conference. The Association also holds regular regional meetings devoted solely to black bears. One meeting I attended in Maine attracted more than a hundred black-bear experts from the eastern United States and Canada.

If any animal is worth saving as part of our environment, it is the black bear. When the colonists first entered the area that later became the United States, they found a vast wilderness filled with many animals, including the black bear. The black bear, more than most other animals, became associated with the wilderness, because it seldom ventures far from forest or swamp. Today, only a remnant of that untouched wilderness is left, but the black bear survives. When we

". . . it is the spirit of the wilderness." (U.S. Fish and Wildlife Service)

see it, it reminds us not only of the wilderness we have lost but also of what remains. It is the spirit of the wilderness.

As one bear biologist pointed out, we don't have to *see* a black bear to summon up the wilderness. It's enough simply to know that somewhere out beyond the end of the road are the same animals our ancestors knew.

Michael Pelton ended an article he wrote for *The Tennessee Conservationist* with these words:

As ecologists search for "indicator species," "environmental monitors" or "ecological yardsticks" by which to measure man's impact on his environment, they should consider this: Perhaps no other form of flora or fauna better represents wilderness in the wooded Eastern United States than does the black bear. It might be said that "as Eastern wilderness goes, so goes the black bear" and vice versa. Whether or not the black bear is used as an "environmental monitor," I would suggest that if ever a symbol is chosen for the wilderness area of the East, no more appropriate animal exists than the black bear. Certainly it deserves to be more than an etching in an ashtray or a picture on a postcard.

Selected Bibliography

Alt, Gary L. 1977. Home range, annual activity patterns and movements of black bears in northeastern Pennsylvania. M.S. thesis, Pennsylvania State University, University Park, Pennsylvania.

Amstrup, Steven C., and Beecham, John. 1976. Activity patterns of radio-collared black bears in Idaho. *Journal of Wildlife Management* 40(2):340–47.

Bacon, E. S. 1973. Investigation on perception and behavior of the American black bear. Ph.D. thesis, University of Tennessee, Knoxville, Tennessee.

Beecham, John J.; Reynolds, Doyle G.; and Hornocker, Maurice G. 1980. Denning ecology of the black bear in west-central Idaho. Fifth International Conference on Bear Research and Management, at Madison, Wisconsin.

Beeman, Larry E., and Pelton, Michael R. 1977. Seasonal foods and food ecology of the black bear in the Smoky Mountains. Fourth International Conference on Bear Research and Management, at Kalispell, Montana.

Burk, Dale, ed. 1979. *The black bear in modern North America.* Clinton, New Jersey: Boone and Crockett Club and Amwell Press.

Cardoza, James E. 1976. *The history and status of the black bear in Massachusetts and adjacent New England states.* Westborough: Massachusetts Division of Fisheries and Wildlife.

Cella, William B., and Keay, Jeffrey A. 1979. *Annual bear management and incident report.* In-house report, Resources Management Division, Yosemite National Park, California.

Cole, Glenn F. 1976. Management involving grizzly and black

bears in Yellowstone National Park 1970–75. *Natural Resources Report Number 9.* Washington, D.C.: U.S. Department of Interior, National Park Service.

Conley, Richard, and Pelton, Michael R., eds. 1974. *Proceedings of the second eastern workshop on black bear management and research, at Gatlinburg, Tennessee.* Nashville: Tennessee Wildlife Resources Agency.

Craighead, John J. and Frank C.; Varney, Joel R.; and Cote, Charles E. 1971. Satellite monitoring of black bear. *Bioscience* 21(24):1206–11.

Dorrance, Michael J., and Gunson, John R. 1976. *An evaluation of nonlethal control techniques for problem black bears in beeyards.* Edmonton: Alberta Agriculture–Plant Industry Laboratory and Alberta Fish and Wildlife Division.

Drucker, Philip. 1963. *Indians of the northwest coast.* Garden City, New York: Natural History Press.

East, Ben. 1977. *Bears.* New York: Outdoor Life–Times Mirror Magazine, Inc.

Erickson, Albert W., Nellor, John, and Petrides, George A. 1964. The black bear in Michigan. Michigan State University, East Lansing, Michigan.

Folk, G. Edgar, Jr. 1967. Physiological observations of subarctic bears under winter den conditions. In *Mammalian Hibernation III*, edited by Kenneth C. Fisher et al. Oliver & Boyd, Ltd.

Folk, G. Edgar, Jr.; Hunt, Jill M.; and Folk, Mary A. 1977. Hibernating bears: further evidence and bioenergetics. Fourth International Conference on Bear Research and Management, at Kalispell, Montana.

Garschulis, D. L. 1978. Movement ecology and activity behavior of black bears in the Great Smoky Mountains National Park. M.S. thesis, University of Tennessee, Knoxville, Tennessee.

Graber, David. 1979. Yosemite's bears. *Bear Biology Association Newsletter.* No. 4:7–8.

Hamilton, Robert J., and Marchinton, R. Larry. 1977. Denning activity of black bears in the coastal plain of North Carolina.

Fourth International Conference on Bear Research and Management, at Kalispell, Montana.

Hamilton, Robert J. 1978. Ecology of the black bear in southeastern North Carolina. M.S. thesis, University of Georgia, Athens, Georgia.

Harms, Dale R. 1977. Black bear management in Yosemite National Park. Fifty-seventh Annual Conference of Western Association of State Game and Fish Commissioners, at Tucson, Arizona.

Henry, J. D., and Herrero, S. M. 1974. Social play in the American black bear: Its similarity to canid social play and an examination of its identifying characteristics. *Am. Zool.* 14:371–91.

Herrero, Stephen. 1970. A black bear and her cub. *Animals.* 12(10):444–47.

Herrero, Stephen, ed. 1972. *Bears — their biology and management: Papers and proceedings of the international conference on bear research and management at Calgary, Alberta, Canada.* Morges, Switzerland: International Union for Conservation of Nature and Natural Resources.

Hugie, Roy D., ed. 1978. *Proceedings of the fourth eastern black bear workshop, at Greenville, Maine.* Augusta: Maine Department of Inland Fisheries and Wildlife.

Hudson, Charles. 1976. *The southeastern Indians.* Knoxville: University of Tennessee Press.

Kammermeyer, Kent. 1979. Stalking the backyard bear. *Outdoors in Georgia.* May:21–26.

Jonkel, Charles J., and Cowan, Ian McT. 1971. *The black bear in the spruce-fir forest.* Washington, D.C. The Wildlife Society, Inc.

Jonkel, Charles. 1979. Habitat. *Bear Biology Association Newsletter.* No. 2–3:1–2.

LaFollette, Julie D. 1974. Some aspects of the history of the black bear in the Great Smoky Mountains. M.S. thesis, University of Tennessee, Knoxville, Tennessee.

Landers, J. Larry, Hamilton, Robert J., Johnson, A. Sydney, and Marchinton, R. Larry. 1979. Food and habitat of black bears in southeastern North Carolina. *Journal of Wildlife Management* 43(1):143–53.

LeCount, Albert, ed. 1979. *Proceedings of the first western black bear workshop, at Tempe, Arizona.* Phoenix: Arizona Game and Fish Department.

LeCount, Albert. 1979. Some bear facts. *Wildlife Views.* 22(2):4–5.

McKinley, Daniel. 1962. History of the black bear in Missouri. *The Bluebird* 29(3):1–16.

Matson, J. R. 1954. Observations on the dormant phase of a female black bear. *Journal of Mammalogy* 35(1):28–35.

Matula, G. J. 1974. Behavioral and physiological characteristics of black bears in northeastern Pennsylvania. M.S. thesis, Pennsylvania State University, University Park, Pennsylvania.

Miller, Robert L. 1971–72. Wild bears in the Catskills. *The Conservationist.* December–January.

Miller, Robert L., ed. 1972. *Proceedings of the 1972 black bear conference at Delmar, New York.* Albany: New York State Department of Environmental Conservation.

Nelson, Ralph A. 1973. Winter sleep in the black bear. *Mayo Clinic Proceedings* 48:733–37.

Pelton, Michael R., Lentfer, Jack W., and Folk, G. Edgar, 1976. *Bears — their biology and management: Papers of the third international conference on bear research and management at Binghamton, New York.* Morges, Switzerland: International Union for Conservation of Nature and Natural Resources.

Pelton, Michael R., Beeman, Larry E., and Eager, Daniel C. 1977. Den selection by black bears in the Great Smoky Mountains National Park. Fourth International Conference on Bear Management and Research, at Kalispell, Montana.

Pelton, Michael R. 1977. The black bear of the smokies. *Tennessee Conservationist* 43(8):12–15.

Piekielek, William, and Burton, Timothy S. 1975. A black bear population study in northern California. *California Fish and Game* 61(1):4–25.

Poelker, Richard J., and Hartwell, Harry D. 1973. *Black bear of*

Washington. Olympia, Washington: Washington State Game Department.

Reynolds, Doyle C. 1977. Home range activities and reproduction of black bears in west-central Idaho. M.S. thesis, University of Idaho, Moscow, Idaho.

Reynolds, Edward E. 1977. An unusual muscle development occurring in the black bear and the raccoon. Fourth International Conference on Bear Research and Management, at Kalispell, Montana.

Rich, Mark. 1976. Bluegenes and Yakutat Barry. *Zoonooz.* June: 9–10.

Rieffenberger, Joe. ed. 1976. *Proceedings of the third eastern black bear workshop at Hershey, Pennsylvania.* Charleston: West Virginia Department of Natural Resources.

Ritzenthaler, Robert E. and Pat. 1970. *The Woodland Indians.* Garden City, New York: Natural History Press.

Rogers, Lynn L. 1977. Social relationships, movements and population dynamics of black bears in northeastern Minnesota. Ph.D. thesis, University of Minnesota, Minneapolis, Minnesota. Ann Arbor, Michigan: University Microfilms International.

Rogers, Lynn L. 1977. Color changes in black bears. Fourth International Conference on Bear Research and Management, at Kalispell, Montana.

Schorger, A. W. 1949. The black bear in early Wisconsin. *Trns. Wis. Acad. Sci. Arts Lett.* 39:151–94.

Steinbock, José Ann. 1978. The war against the animals. *Matrix.* Fall:14–15.

Steinhart, Peter. 1978. Getting to know bruin better. *National Wildlife.* 16(5):20–27.

Stewart, T. D. 1959. Bear paw remains closely resemble human bones. *FBI Law Enforcement Bulletin.* November:18–21.

Tyler, Hamilton A. 1975. *Pueblo animals and myths.* Norman: University of Oklahoma Press.

Underhill, Ruth M. 1965. *Red man's religion.* Chicago: University of Chicago Press.

Van Wormer, Joe. 1966. *World of the black bear.* Philadelphia: J. B. Lippincott.

Whitlock, S. C. 1950. The black bear as a predator of man. *Journal of Mammalogy* 31(2):135–37.

Willey, Charles H. 1974. Aging black bears from first premolar tooth sections. *Journal of Wildlife Management* 38(1):97–100.

Willey, Charles H. 1978. *The Vermont black bear.* Montpelier: Vermont Fish and Game Department.

Index